Remember the Magic...

The Story of Horizon Air

Bill Endicott

TURNER PUBLISHING COMPANY

Library of Congress Control Number:
2001091500

Turner Publishing Company Staff:
Dayna Spear Williams, Editor
Shelley R. Davidson, Designer

ISBN 978-1-68162-338-2

Additional copies may be purchased
directly from the publisher.

Contents

"Make no little plans;

they have no magic to stir men's blood."

Daniel Hudson Burnham 1846-1912

Dedicated to the memory of original
Horizon team members:

Kathy Anderson Kuolt
Scott Kidwell
Dewaine Wall
John Cox
Frank Bryant

Acknowledgments

My deepest thanks to former and current employees of Horizon Air for sharing their memories. This is their story.

Thanks, too, to those who are now with Alaska Air Group and Alaska Airlines. Their timely acquisition of Horizon Air in 1987 resulted in the airline remaining a truly Northwest airline. With Alaska's nurturing and support, Horizon continues its successful flight into the new century.

My personal gratitude to Sandra Mitchell, Milt Kuolt's administrative assistant, without whose efforts this book could not have been written. And Milt Kuolt — whose encouragement and candor allowed the truth to be told. To Bruce McCaw, who because of his flawless memory for detail and factual events, made a major contribution to this book.

While working with Milt and the media on a daily basis from Thousand Trails in 1977 through Alaska's acquisition of Horizon in 1987, there was never a dull moment. On a slow news day, I could expect a call from someone wanting to interview Milt. Believe me, that usually spiced up the day considerably. Milt could always be counted on to provide something worthy of a sound bite. In today's environment of political correctness and diversity, Milt's outspoken honesty on any subject would not fly but then neither would Horizon Air. His boldness by word and deed is the cornerstone of his business successes. Milt's views and management techniques may seem unorthodox to some observers, but they proved to be the very elements that created one of America's most successful regional airlines.

This book has been three years in the writing. Interviews with over 100 people can mean that one person may remember the magic in a different way from another. I have tried to give an honest account of events from my own experience and from the information provided by others. Quoted remarks are the sole responsibility of the person who provided the quote.

Introduction

June 9, 1940, thirteen-year-old Milton Kuolt II searched his parent's faces for the same bursting exuberance he felt in his own heart. *Are we really here? Is this America?* Crowded by the hundreds of other eager passengers at the rail of the ship, *The Nita Maru,* as it passed under the Golden Gate, young Milton had just gotten his first glimpse of The United States of America and it took his breath away. This was the homeland of his parents, Rev. Milton and Martha Kuolt. This was the land of the free and home of the brave! The boy had loved listening to his parent's stories about America and he had read more about it at the mission school. Lutheran missionaries, Rev. and Mrs. Kuolt were returning with their children on furlough from Ambur in southern India. Milt, his brother John and his two sisters, Julie and Margie had all been born in India.

Rev. and Mrs. Kuolt watched their son, Milton, as they shared that magic moment together. Seeing his face illuminated with joy as he saw with his own eyes this heretofore mythical, imagined land of freedom and promise, they had no way of knowing that they were introducing to their country one of the great entrepreneurs of the Twentieth Century.

The Reverend and Mrs. Kuolt with their children in India. Milt Kuolt, front center, is flanked by his sisters Julie and Margie. His younger brother, John, is between their parents.

About a year and a half after the family's return to the States, on December 8, 1941, America declared war with the Japanese. Unable to return to the mission field, the Kuolts first made their home in Webster Grove, Missouri and later in Philadelphia. There, young Milton enrolled in Llanerch High School where his classmates voted him "least likely to succeed." Milton was to use that judgment as an incentive in the years to come.

Four months before graduation in 1945, Milt enlisted in the Navy where he served eighteen months. Upon discharge, he enrolled in the Bartlett School of Tree Surgery in Stamford, Connecticut, after which he embarked upon his first entrepreneurial enterprise with a high school buddy. This first venture was known as "Gunther and Kuolt, Tree Expert Company." He didn't make his first million as a tree surgeon but that acquired skill was to pave the way to his higher education.

Milt went west in 1948, seeking a wrestling scholarship at San Diego State University. So he could "beef up," the coach suggested he get a job in the woods.

He found work as a choker setter with Weyerhaeuser at Castle Rock, Washington. After hurting his leg on the second day of work, he decided the risk wasn't worth it. He abruptly quit and hitchhiked to Seattle, bought a bus ticket to Ellensburg, and enrolled in Central Washington State College, now a university.

Photo courtesy of Washington CEO *magazine.*

Low on funds, Milt pondered the huge number of maple and elm trees abounding on campus. He used his GI Bill benefits and bartered with school officials to help him pay the balance for his college degree. Milt's idea was tuition for work, and he convinced the school to hire him for all tree maintenance on the sprawling campus – at four times the going rate paid a student worker.

Economics degree in hand, Milt devoted the next twenty years to The Boeing Company where he started as a storekeeper/janitor, then moved to facilities planning and layout. He rose to the position of business planning manager of the 737 program. In his second decade with Boeing, Milt developed an interest in owning land and land development with a view toward capital appreciation and the value of land as a non-liquid asset. That interest resulted in an idea for a private campground concept and

Thousand Trails was born. Trails became one of the most successful outdoor campground companies in America. Milt took the company to $40 million in annual revenues and then turned it over to others to take it to $100 million plus.

Along the way, Milt gained an understanding of the air travel club concept when he was introduced to the locally-based Argosy Flying Club. Argosy was later sold to a Denver entity but that exposure led to the idea of creating a new airline.

By mid-1980, Milt Kuolt, frustrated with marginal airline service, lost luggage and late arrivals, drew together men and women to help him with his dream of creating a new regional airline. Joe Clark provided the stimulus in the early discussions. Horizon Air quickly became the Number One choice of business travelers and, in six years, became one of the top six regional airlines in the country.

This book chronicles that adventure from beginning until acquisition by the Alaska Air Group. All of it is true. It is a testimony to the vision, courage and skills of one man, Milt Kuolt. Inside this man is the heart of a lion. He knows who he is and makes neither boast nor apology. His business successes and generosity have enriched the lives of millions, individually and collectively. Milt has never lost his compassion for the less fortunate. His philanthropies range from anonymously helping the down and out in America to supporting an orphanage in Mexico.

Milt Kuolt thrives on the adventure of new ideas and the process of entrepreneurship that has made America great. He draws the good and the exceptional people to him with a magnetism that has nothing to do with his IQ or wealth.

He's a winner.

"I don't like following the pack. It's really quite boring and the view is lousy from back there. Get out front with your ideas and have the drive and conviction to make them happen. That's the magic of success."

Join me now as we remember the magic that was and is Horizon Air.

Bill Endicott

𝒯𝒽𝑒 𝒫𝓁𝒶𝓎𝑒𝓇𝓈

Milt Kuolt. It was his dream and he made it a reality. Milt confounds his critics and rewards his supporters. He motivates, is a relentless entrepreneur, an unheralded philanthropist, outspoken critic and most of all, *numero uno* role model for anyone seeking to venture into the unknown.

"The Grinder"

Bruce McCaw. The steadying influence in Milt Kuolt's adventurous forays. A lifelong aviation buff who pilots his Lear 35 and Falcon 900 jets, he is active in organizations supporting aviation and children's charities. He has a passion for racing cars and is an avid collector of automotive

"McCoo"

memorabilia and classic motorcars. Bruce serves as Vice Chariman/Trustee for the Museum of Flight.

Joe Clark. Founder of three aviation-based enterprises: Jet Air, Avstar, Inc. and Aviation Partners, Inc. At Horizon, Joe was the airline's first executive and first VP of sales and marketing. Additionally, he was responsible for special projects and served as a director on Horizon's board.

"Sun Valley Joe"

He is a Trustee for Seattle's Museum of Flight.

Tom Cufley. The classic birdman. From the time his dad bought him a plane ride as a kid to captaining an Alaska Airlines MD-80, Tom contributed his skills and charm to the industry. Under stress at Horizon, Tom's professionalism and cheerful demeanor helped make it all work. With 20,000 flying hours and 25 years in aviation, he is retired.

"El Supremo"

Dianna Maul. If Dee Dee's many attributes were condensed into one title, it would be "Ms. Customer Service." In the early days, it was just Dee Dee and Kathy Anderson. When the airline was sold six years later with 1100 employees in 37 cities in nine states, customer service was a major contributing factor to Horizon's success.

"Dee Dee"

Alan Zanouzoski. Alan joined Horizon initially as chief pilot, director of training and director of flight operations. He was the "hard-nosed" professional who demanded the highest level of pilot training and efficiency. With Cufley, Alan created Horizon's first flight operations manual.

"Z"

Richard W. Heaton. You break 'em, Dick fixes 'em. This not only applies to all types of aircraft but to all his neighbor's engines where he and Audrey live at Hood Canal, WA. A real pro and a no-nonsense airframe and powerplant expert, Dick's team kept Horizon's planes running, maintained and on line for scheduled departures.

"Father Heaton"

Kathy Anderson Kuolt. Kathy's charm, wit and sparkling personality put the class into Horizon's customer service. After becoming Milt's wife, she continued her considerable contributions to the airline's success. Since her untimely death in 1998, Kathy is deeply missed by all who knew and loved her.

"Kathy"

H.A. "Andy" Andersen. Andy came to Horizon's board from Air Oregon's board in acquisition. Founder and chairman of Andersen Construction Company, he is responsible for many innovative achievements in his industry. Aviation has played a major role in Andy's life. And, more than once, he helped rescue Horizon from near-financial disaster.

"The Angel"

George Bagley. George joined Horizon when the carrier acquired Transwestern Airlines of Utah in 1983. From senior VP of operations, George was elected president of Horizon in 1995. A former Air Force pilot, he holds a BS degree in aeronautics from Utah State University and is a licensed airframe and powerplant mechanic.

"Bag"

John R. Kuolt. Sales and marketing were John's niche. His sales team would swoop into a new city targeted for service and blitz the market. This image enhancement built awareness with tens of thousands of passengers. The strategy for getting people out of their cars and onto the airplane was highly successful.

"John"

Bill Ayer. Bill has risen steadily through the ranks. Beginning as director of sales and marketing at Horizon in 1982, in the new millennium, he is president of Alaska Airlines. He has an MBA from the University of Washington and holds commercial and flight instructor certificates with instrument and multi-engine ratings.

"Air"

Don Welsh. Just 22 and working for United, Don jumped at the opportunity to join Horizon. He quickly developed the carrier's first sales and marketing plan that met both the competitive challenge and established Horizon as the Northwest's dominant regional carrier.

"Game Face"

Mel Kays. Mel always knew where the bucks were internally and where they could be found externally. He came from a major accounting firm to Thousand Trails and later to Horizon. Never one to yell or scream, his professionalism was a leveler during turbulent times. Today, Mel is executive VP and CFO with GlobeNet.

"Kays"

Bill Endicott. Founder of a Northwest PR firm in the early 70s, and a pilot since WWII, Bill began working with Milt at Thousand Trails in investor relations and was a consultant to Horizon from day one. He also served in a key role working with media in every city Horizon served and considers the years with Horizon a highlight of his professional career.

"Wild Bill"

Mike Lowry. Mike came from a major accounting firm to Horizon as controller, then moved to VP of finance.

He was also involved with other team members in evaluating Ponderosa as a potential acquisition prior to Horizon's debut. Today, Mike is an integral part of the PacWest Auto Racing team.

"Shade"

David Sawyer. Adept at mining cash in reluctant bankers' pockets, Sawyer is also equally recognized by myriad companies for vastly improving their accounts receivable and cash flow. He was a co-founder and is now president of The Coffee Station, Inc.

"Sawyer"

Don Streun. As an Air Oregon director, Don joined Horizon with the 1982 acquisition. Highly respected for his insight and cool demeanor, Don made significant contributions to Horizon's business success. He was a master at the art of give and take with Milt Kuolt.

"Streun"

The Dream - Will It Fly?

"Oh, my God! You call that an airplane?"

At the sight of what was to be the first of three aircraft in the fleet for Horizon Air, Bruce McCaw thought Milt Kuolt was going to collapse. On a spring day in 1981, the pair had waited at Boeing Field until four in the afternoon for the long overdue F-27 to show up. They had small-talked through the arduous hours, all the while casting nervous glances out the window to Runway 13 Right. Other tense observers involved in the plan were Kathy Anderson, Dee Dee Maul, Joe Clark and Dick Heaton. They were gathered in the Blue Max Restaurant, atop Boeing Field's main terminal in Seattle. Now, the wait was over. Milt, well fortified with rum and cokes during the vigil, bolted toward the door, followed by a near mass exodus of Blue Max patrons.

"Let's get a look at this piece of junk!" Kuolt muttered as he quickly descended from the terminal's top deck.

It was Tom Cufley and Bruce McRae's job to pick up the recently overhauled Fairchild F-27 in Montreal and bring it to its new home in Seattle. Cufley had been chief pilot for Hughes Airwest F-27 operations for Saudi Arabian Airlines. Bruce McRae, who had been

Tom Cufley

Kuolt's personal pilot at Thousand Trails was already on board when he located Cufley. Cufley had taken a leave of absence pending the acquisition of Hughes

Bruce McRae

Airwest by Republic Airlines and he was flying night freight out of Boeing Field in a DC-3. Cufley had never heard of Milt Kuolt so McRae prepared him to meet with the founder. He started his profile of Kuolt with a tongue-in-cheek statement, "You know we have to be pretty careful because Milt is a very religious man."

Off they went to the Horizon office at the south end of SeaTac on 188th Street where Cufley got his introduction to Milt Kuolt. Keeping in mind McRae's cautions, he was stunned to see Kuolt dashing here and there in the office, hollering expletives. Cufley recalled, "I was like a wild-eyed deer caught in a headlight."

But it wasn't long into Milt's briefing that Cufley caught the vision. And Kuolt liked the fact that for four years, Cufley had been chief pilot for Cascade Airways which gave him experience flying established routes over the Cascade Mountains. Kuolt told him he was hired, adding, "Show me what you can do. That's what I need to see."

One of Cufley's early priorities was to contact Alan Zanouzoski, with whom he had flown night freight for United Parcel Service. Milt approved "Z," bringing him aboard as Chief Pilot and Director of Training. Tom was Director of Flight Operations. The two men were an ideal blend of talents; Alan, the perfectionist, insisting on training at the highest level and Tom, the cool head and diplomat who kept things light. Among early pilots Tom hired were Gerry Vanderville, Jim Dupenthaler, Larry Vogel, Bruce McRae, Bob Stanton, Jerry Knaust and Randy Malquist. Several had been captains flying F-27s with Tom in Saudi, Arabia and had a strong team mentality when joining Horizon.

On his layovers in Spokane with the United Parcel Service DC-3, Cufley, together with Zanouzoski, began writing the flight manual for Horizon which at that time was called Pacific Horizon. The "Pacific" was dropped when Kuolt reasoned that it was too geographically limiting.

Bruce McRae had been one of Cufley's first officers in the desert when the project shut down in the early 1980's. Both in their early forties, each man looked as trim as the typical fighter jock from World War II. The taller McRae's handlebar mustache gave him the appearance of an officer in the RAF. Cufley's genial demeanor and chief pilot experience earned for him a leadership role with the fledgling airline.

"I got the weather report." Cufley reflected recently on the very important delivery of the first aircraft to launch the fledgling airline – and the first F-27 flight to Boeing Field. "It looked pretty good for most of the trip except for some low cloud cover in Montreal. Preflight inspection went fine. Gear, control surfaces, props all checked out. We pulled the cabin door shut and wound our way toward the cockpit through heaps of spare parts that were strapped to the deck."

The spare parts took up most of the cabin where passenger seats once were anchored. The F-27 was close to maximum weight for the aircraft. Completing the cockpit checklist, they cranked the right engine of the turboprop. Then the left. All instrument readouts appeared normal for the old bird. Cleared to taxi and take off, they began the climb to 24,000 feet, their initial cruise altitude.

About five minutes out and still in the clouds, suddenly McRae shouted: "Sonofabitch, look at this!" The plane had totally lost alternating current electrical power. Not just partial. Total. The only instruments operating were the plane's whiskey compass, a pilot's term for the gyro compass that floats in alcohol, turn and bank indicator and the aircraft radios.

Cool as an iced Coors, Cufley climbed through 10,000 feet and the thick cloud layer into clear skies. McRae took the controls and Cufley headed back to the electrical panel. He began removing and replacing components, resetting circuit breakers and was finally able to restore full power to the cockpit instrument display. In the interim, they had been literally flying an IFR flight plan without instruments.

Back in control, Cufley lit up the cockpit with a relaxed grin. He felt like one of the fearless pilots who flew the U.S. Mail in the late nineteen twenties in their Travel Airs.

He lived for this. What else was there? Cocking his head in McRae's direction, Cufley exclaimed, "Milt's gonna love this!"

One thing was for certain. Milt Kuolt had once again selected the right men for the job. If the airline's founder had been on board for this unexpected electrical scare, he would have gained a real appreciation for the competency of his pilots.

There were refueling stops at Thunder Bay, on Canada's northern shores of Lake Superior and Regina, Saskatchewan where they topped off with Jet A fuel. Clearing customs would take place at their final destination.

Back in Seattle, at about the time Cufley and McRae were taking off in Montreal, Milt Kuolt received an early morning call from Bruce McCaw.

"Just got a call from Tom and they expect to be in here around two this afternoon."

There was silence on the other end of the line.

"Are you there?" McCaw asked.

"Yeah." Kuolt hesitated. "You think we're doing the right thing? (pause) I mean, do you think this will really fly?"

Bruce McCaw realized what was happening. Milt's uneasiness was not about this aircraft. He was questioning his decision to start up a regional airline. His friend was having perfectly normal, natural doubts about yet another one of his ideas. McCaw recognized the symptoms having worked with Milt on other projects. Their friendship is sometimes akin to a Mexican standoff since both men have strong opinions and no hesitation voicing them, but they understand each other. McCaw waited a beat, then patiently settled his partner down and brought him back to focus.

"Milt, these planes are fresh out of overhaul. And for what we paid for them, I don't think we could have done better. So meet me at the Blue Max. We'll have some lunch. There will be several of us watching for them. Come on. This is the day!"

This was the day all right. And this was plane number one? This beater?

Milt and company rushed out onto the ramp as the aircraft slowed to a stop. It didn't get any better up close. The F-27 hadn't been painted in any recent year. Not quite like the jury-rigged C-119 that Jimmy Stewart flew in the movie "The Flight of the Phoenix," but close.

Everybody kept his or her thoughts to themselves. This was going to work. They would all see to it. Customs met and cleared the plane where it stopped.

UNITED STATES OF AMERICA
U.S. DEPARTMENT OF TRANSPORTATION
FEDERAL AVIATION ADMINISTRATION

Air Carrier Operating Certificate

This certifies that

HORIZON AIRLINES, INC., D/B/A
HORIZON AIR
7887 PERIMETER ROAD SOUTH
SEATTLE, WASHINGTON   98108

has met the requirements of the Federal Aviation Act of 1958, as amended, and the rules, regulations, and standards prescribed thereunder for the issuance of this certificate, and is hereby authorized to operate as an air carrier in accordance with said Act and the rules, regulations and standards prescribed thereunder, and the terms, conditions, and limitations contained in the operations specifications.

This certificate is not transferable and, unless sooner surrendered, suspended or revoked, shall continue in effect indefinitely.

By Direction of the Administrator

Certificate number: __NW-2__

Effective date: AUGUST 31, 1981

Issued at: SEATTLE, WASHINGTON

HAL W. MORRILL
(Signature)

CHIEF, NW-FSDO-61
(Title)

FAA FORM 8430-16 (3-79)

The Impact of Deregulation

I t is important to understand the culture of the airline industry in 1981 that allowed Horizon's entry. For years, the Civil Aeronautics Board, (CAB) had been the economic authority governing civil aviation, determining which airlines would fly, to where and what they would charge their passengers. It was typical government regulation that stifles the entrepreneur for whom anything regulatory and bureaucratic was anathema. When Deregulation came in 1978, it spelled the demise of many air travel clubs that had enjoyed a competitive niche in the industry under the protection of the regulatory body.

Major carriers didn't immediately discern what was about to happen to their industry. For many, it was business as usual because for so long, they had operated under the protective arm of the Federal government. Passengers were frequently treated with indifference and passenger service was secondary to passenger revenues.

None of this escaped Milt Kuolt's attention.

At the end of 1978, large U.S. certificated airlines served a total of 473 airports in 49 states and the District of Columbia. When Deregulation took effect, service to smaller communities by the larger carriers decreased as the larger carriers sought more profitable markets. However, the medium and smaller-sized markets did not lose service, as regional and commuter carriers filled the gap left by the larger carrier's exits. In the first twenty years since Deregulation, the number of communities receiving service exclusively from regional and commuter carriers increased from 112 to 399.

In the process, some smaller communities initially lost air service entirely. This was remedied when Congress added Section 419 to the Federal Aviation Act, which established the Essential Air Service Program, which ensured smaller communities a link to the national air transportation system, with Federal subsidy when necessary. When the program was started, there were 383 points receiving subsidies. By May of 1998, there were but 104 communities receiving the subsidy, 26 of those located in Alaska.

Since passage of the Airline Deregulation Act in 1978, *regional* airline revenue passenger miles (RPMs) have increased an average of over fourteen percent a year. The vision at the time was that both the air carrier industry and the traveling public would benefit from Deregulation. More than twenty years have passed and, for the most part, it appears to have accomplished its purpose. The success of Horizon Air is living proof.

First flight, September 1, 1981.

Milt's Introduction to Aviation

It didn't take Milt long after reaching the shores of the United States in 1940 to become the typical American youth of that era, including building balsa wood model airplanes.

"And I flew them, too!" he adds. *Of course.*

Fast forward to 1980. Milt was in Dallas, meeting with investors of Thousand Trails, his publicly-held company. He asked Bill Endicott, who was then investor relations counsel for Trails, "What would you think if I started up an airline?" Bill's response was quick and direct. "Milt, what do you know about running an airline?"

"Hell, it's nothing but providing service to people!" Milt burst out in typical fashion. "And from what I've seen,

Bill Endicott and Milt Kuolt at the founders' 15th Anniversary get-together in Puerto Vallarta.

today's airlines don't really grasp what service is all about. The technical stuff, like pilots and maintenance, is the easy side but the service side is what will make us different. The carriers out there have a cavalier attitude toward their passengers. They give little thought to what happens to either their baggage or their travel plans. Most of these airline CEOs think flying airplanes is their business, when in fact, the only thing you have to sell is service. The technical part of running an airline is easy. It's the art form that makes the difference."

That was good enough for Bill. His respect for Milt's business acumen and judgment has never been shaken.

He put his hands in the air, saying, "Well, Chief, you've convinced me!"

Bruce McCaw says the beginning of Horizon actually predates Milt's declaration that December day in Dallas by more than a decade. The year was 1969 when McCaw, Chuck Jones and pilot Scott Kidwell, who was on furlough from West Coast Airlines, were involved with the Argosy Air Travel Club. McCaw was a board member and Scott and Chuck were pilot/executives.

In 1969 Milt was totally focused on The Pacific Rim Group, a land syndication company, which was a popular thing at the time and the predecessor of Thousand Trials. Following an introduction to Kuolt, McCaw joined with Kuolt and twenty or so other investors to purchase land near Chehalis, Washington, which later became the nucleus for Thousand Trails. This was a business Kuolt was running out of his house while still employed by Boeing.

Kidwell, Jones and McCaw talked Kuolt into becoming involved with Argosy and Milt, the campground CEO, began to give the travel club direction. As Argosy's situation improved, the club acquired a second DC-7, for which Kuolt paid $25,000. Although Argosy's operation had been moved to Boeing Field, the second aircraft was transferred to Paine Field where it became known as the "parts plane."

Kuolt asked McCaw to take him up to Paine so he could see the airplane his money had bought. Before showing Kuolt the DC-7, McCaw had prepared him for the absence of one engine.

"And where's the fourth engine?"

"Well, we just needed it for the weekend," McCaw explained. By then the DC-7's flying days were nearly over as were Argosy's. The club was sold and moved to Denver.

Subsequently, Kuolt acquired his second property at Cle Elum and several more travel clubs came into being including Sunfari, Club International, Jet Set and others. In the realm of regulations governing different types of air operations, all were known as Part 123 ATC carriers. By 1972, McCaw was involved in insuring travel clubs and had bought a travel agency. The airlines were putting up a lot of flak with the Civil Aeronautics Board because the travel clubs were doing so well, but it gave McCaw an excellent opportunity to learn a great deal about the industry.

As Thousand Trails was beginning to grow, Kuolt approached McCaw several times about integrating an air travel club with campground memberships. He told McCaw, "We've got all these members. Let's start putting them on airplanes."

Scott Kidwell, who was from Yakima, also helped Kuolt evaluate the potential for a new airline. During this time Kuolt was understanding more and more about clubs and the air travel business while still involved with Trails. But just before Thousand Trails went public, the campground company was experiencing some tough financial times. For a period of two to three years, Kuolt was more concerned about nurturing his campground company than any airline venture.

Some of his financial problems were resolved with Trails Initial Public Offering and Kuolt went to McCaw.

"I want to get Thousand Trails an airplane and add it to the club and start flying people to resort destinations."

In the months that followed, the pair investigated the possibility of launching an air travel adjunct to Thousand Trails, but the economics weren't making much sense. With increased scrutiny by the regulators and a prominent air travel club's high visibility bankruptcy, it was determined that they were not ready to venture into this arena. Following Deregulation in 1978, air travel clubs either went into the airline business or disappeared.

Kuolt continued his focus on Thousand Trails but, at McCaw's suggestion, did take time to look at Ponderosa, an undercapitalized Tahoe-based carrier that had a certificate to fly interstate between Tahoe and Seattle/ Portland. Kidwell, McCaw and others were trying to acquire and finance the company. Kuolt wanted to look at using a Boeing 707. Ponderosa was trying to acquire F-28s and Convair 580s. McCaw reflects today that if they had bought Ponderosa just for its airplanes under contract and had done nothing with the operation, they would have "made a couple million bucks." In acquiring Ponderosa, the original plan was to operate it as an interstate carrier, then go to an intrastate operation. Joe Clark, who was involved with McCaw on other projects, was introduced to Milt and asked to explore putting it all together.

The plan was to have Kidwell acquire the airplanes while McCaw would oversee operations. The thinking was that once the interstate operation was up and going, F-27s would be acquired for an operation within Washington State. Remember, this was about four years prior to the actual birth of Horizon.

Scott Kidwell and Milt Kuolt

Take Off

P urchase of the first F-27s ended months of searching for aircraft that would be suitable for Horizon's planned service over the Cascades, initially linking the Washington state cities of Seattle on the West with Yakima and Pasco to the East.

Following exploratory discussions in the mid-70s, the dream came to fruition in early 1980 when Milt Kuolt, Joe Clark, Bruce McCaw and Scott Kidwell met to talk about beginning a new airline. The first idea explored was to fly a Boeing 707 between Seattle and Hawaii. But with a planned $100 fare each way, the idea was discarded. Joe Clark said, "The big carriers like United would squash us like a bug!" After all, Braniff had tried that route, flying from Seattle-Portland to Honolulu with $60 - $70 fares and often with just thirty passengers on a 747, before finally giving it up.

It became apparent that any new carrier's niche was within the state of Washington, competing directly with existing carriers, Republic and Cascade Airways, which was headquartered in Spokane.

Although the dreamers explored the idea of acquiring Cascade Airways, after discussion, that idea was tossed. Then Scott Kidwell advanced the idea of flying pressurized planes between Seattle and Yakima and Seattle and Pasco. After John Cox conducted a market analysis, the team talked the idea through and Horizon Air was launched.

Joe Clark and Kidwell came to Kuolt and told him that *pressurized* aircraft would have to be flown over the Cascade Mountains, as compared to the unpressurized airplanes being flown by Cascade Airways. Kuolt understood. His thinking, though, was that all he would want to serve from Seattle was two markets: Yakima and the Pasco/Tri Cities area. Kuolt envisioned a small staff and three or four flights a day serving two cities with two airplanes. In 1981, he had no plans beyond that or at least none that he discussed.

Later that thinking would be expanded to include Sun Valley, Portland, Spokane and Walla Walla. But, initially, all he wanted to do was start a small airline and to keep it small; his philosophy: "when you're small it's easy to be real good, but the bigger you grow, it's tougher to get better."

While this business venture was being massaged, Thousand Trails, now gaining investor confidence, saw its stock appreciating in value. Kuolt's majority ownership of the campground company would allow him to use some of his Trails stock as collateral to finance the startup. McCaw had assembled a group that would put up the money to finance the aircraft. But the timing was not right. This was the period immediately before the Deregulation of airlines. Undaunted, Kuolt then wanted to explore the potential for long-haul routes. McCaw sat him down.

"Milt, if you do that, you'll lose your ass!"

"Why?" Kuolt demanded.

"Because the yields are so low. Remember what happened to Braniff!"

The thinking now went full circle and the team was taking another look at short-haul routes. A business plan was drafted for a short-haul airline. *McCaw says that is when the team really started focusing on creating a regional carrier.*

Hangar space had been acquired for the refurbishing of the first aircraft and all other F-27s to follow as soon as deals could be made. Scott Kidwell searched for available used aircraft that flew but needed a little refurbishing. Scouting trips were made to Africa, Bolivia, Peru and other points in South America.

Horizon's future Vice President of Maintenance, Dick Heaton, was a longtime friend of McCaw, going back to the air travel clubs. McCaw knew that just as Cufley was expert at flying F-27s, Heaton was expert at maintaining them.

SCHEDULE EFFECTIVE
SEPTEMBER 1, 1981 FOR YAKIMA
SEPTEMBER 7, 1981 FOR PASCO

RESERVATIONS
SEATTLE (SEA) 762-3646
YAKIMA (YKM) 1-800-562-8850
PASCO (PSC) 1-800-562-8850

MONDAY THRU FRIDAY

SEATTLE to YAKIMA				YAKIMA to SEATTLE			
Leave	Arrive	Flight	Stops	Leave	Arrive	Flight	Stops
7:30 am	8:10 am	100	0	8:30 am	9:10 am	101	0
*10:00 am	10:40 am	200	0	*11:00 am	11:40 am	201	0
4:30 pm	5:10 pm	108	0	5:30 pm	6:10 pm	109	0
7:00 pm	7:40 pm	116	0	* 8:00 pm	8:40 pm	217	0
*10:30 pm	11:10 pm	212	0				

SEATTLE to PASCO				PASCO to SEATTLE			
Leave	Arrive	Flight	Stops	Leave	Arrive	Flight	Stops
7:00 am	7:55 am	170	0	6:15 am	7:10 am	133	0
9:35 am	10:30 am	130	0	8:20 am	9:15 am	171	0
* 4:00 pm	4:55 pm	230	0	*10:50 am	11:45 am	233	0
7:15 pm	8:10 pm	140	0	5:30 pm	6:25 pm	143	0
*10:30 pm	11:55 pm	212	YKM	* 8:30 pm	9:25 pm	263	0

YAKIMA to PASCO			
Leave	Arrive	Flight	Stops
*11:30 pm	11:55 pm	*212	0

First Horizon Timetable

was expert at maintaining them.

Heaton was visited at his Boeing Field office and, after McCaw encouraged Dick to consider Horizon's offer, Heaton said, "Well, you got here at the right time. I just had a couple a shootouts with my boss."

"I don't see any bullet holes," McCaw said with a wide grin.

"That's because I'm fast on my feet!" Both men laughed. Heaton next had a talk with Milt and, during his interview, was hired.

Dick Heaton was concerned about purchasing the spare parts required to maintain the fleet. His answer came when Kidwell located three F-27s at Quebec Air in Canada, *with spares*. He found the aircraft through a Florida broker, Clyde Mash, who had an exclusive on the planes.

Seafirst Bank provided a line of credit. The first three aircraft were to be secured with about $3 million in Horizon stock, amounting to around $800,000 per airplane plus another $600,000 for spare parts.

The plan was cast in concrete with a September 1, 1981 launch date and it was Horizon Air's "takeoff roll." Cufley was hired as director of flight operations and Alan Zanouzoski, a former flying partner of Cufley, was chief pilot and director of training. Tom also had the responsibility to get a Part 121 operating certificate from the FAA to begin flying. Part 121 designation governs air operations for commercial aircraft, transport category, weighing in excess of 12,500 pounds. Heaton was to oversee the total refurbishing, painting and rollout of each aircraft.

Dianna "Dee Dee" Maul was responsible for setting up the stations and customer service department. Reservations, ticketing and hiring of necessary personnel to staff the positions followed shortly thereafter. Others were involved in ensuring handlers were on the ramp to move baggage and to staff the corporate office with accounting and other support personnel.

Marian Clark, the first Horizon employee hired. (Now Marian Clark Cufley)

The Magic Begins

Anear miracle took place when Tom Cufley was able to get Horizon's Part 121 operating certificate from the FAA in less than 70 days. This was unheard of. The certificate was awarded to Horizon Air *one day* before the first scheduled passenger service. Normally, an application took from six months to a year to wind its way through the bureaucratic process. With his patented grin, Cufley explained, "Just a little magic."

Another necessary element for start-up was a three-letter identifier for the airline. Since the planes were to be picked up in Montreal, that was where the identifier had to be issued. Cufley went to the International Civil Aviation Organization (ICAO) office in Montreal. There he told the attractive young lady at the desk that he represented a new airline in the Pacific Northwest and his mission was to get the three-letter identifier.

The attractive young lady asked Cufley what letters he had in mind. He told her E P H. "Fine," she said. "You should have your identifier in about six months."

"No, no, no! You don't understand," Cufley said softly between clenched teeth. "I need this identifier within the next two days. I have to take it back *with* me. We're starting this airline up in three weeks."

"No, no, no, Mr. Cufley," she gently reminded him. "It takes a long time to get an identifier."

"But I can't go back without the letters," he implored. The conversation went back and forth while the attractive young lady remained stoic. Cufley, completely frustrated, turned a half circle toward the door, then whirled back around to the desk and blurted out,

"Are you married?"

"No," she said, looking up, wide-eyed at Cufley.

"Why?"

"I tell you what." And he flashed that irresistible smile.

"How about we go out on the town tonight in Montreal? We'll get a limo and do the whole nine yards, dinner, a show. Money is no object." *After all, it was Milt's money.*

"Really?" She exclaimed, suddenly quite animated.

"Absolutely!" Cufley beamed.

The attractive young lady reached down into a drawer under the counter and pulled out a small, official-looking book. After a couple of phone calls to Seattle, Cufley made one local call – for a limo. The identifier problem had been solved. Tom remembers that the pair went to a place called Thursdays and Fridays, actually two old houses downtown separated by a causeway, and he remembers "the food was great!"

Meanwhile, back in Seattle, Horizon Air was beginning to take shape. Bill Lloyd, a creative advertising person moonlighting from Boeing, was hired for $500 to design the Horizon logo and livery. A good investment, the design proved to be a smash hit. A dark red sun on lighter and lighter yellow, then the horizon line and the turquoise color for the sea.

More important than logo was capitalization. Founders put in a combined $3.6 million, with Kuolt contributing two thirds. The four brothers McCaw each put in $50,000. Clark and others put in some more. Early investors also included David and Joyce Adams, ranchers from Eastern Washington who, like McCaw, had invested with Kuolt in Thousand Trails.

Dee Dee Maul learned of the Horizon startup when former Cascade fellow employee, Tom Cufley told her

Horizon was looking for someone to handle stations and customer service. She had put in 13 years with Cascade and the carrier's situation was getting scary. She was ready to bail. Dee Dee described the environment at Cascade as so dismal that anyone with tenure wanted out. There was never any good news and often there was bad news. It had been rumored that

"Dee Dee" Maul

Cascade was missing payroll and was unable to pay vendors and that its employees were seeking to go anywhere that promised some security.

"I had this conversation with Tom Cufley," Maul recalled, "And he said, 'Hey, there is a guy I want you to meet. His name is Joe Clark and he's with this new airline.' So, I set a meeting with Joe and I was a bit nervous since I had been with Cascade for 13 years and had not been actively seeking a change of employment."

Maul walked into what was loosely called his office upstairs in a building at Boeing Field. She remembers a large round table with one phone and clutter everywhere. Joe Clark rose to shake her hand and tripped over a 50-foot long phone cord, nearly landing himself head over teakettle. In the interest of early economies, the single phone had to stretch between two rooms.

Her initial impression was *this is a real klutz!*

Clark invited Maul to lunch and, in his car on the way said, "I've forgotten my wallet. Do you have any money?"

"No, I don't." she said. *Did anyone who worked for Cascade have any money?*

"We'll just stop at my apartment and I'll pick up my wallet. Want to come up?"

"No. I'll just wait in the car." Maul remembers they went to a greasy spoon in the Georgetown area north of Boeing Field. Clark provided an overview of the new airline that left her with the impression that it sounded like a real shady deal. Clark called her the next day, saying, "I want you to meet Milt Kuolt. He's the guy who's running this airline."

Okay. This has to get better!

Maul walked into the hangar where she was to meet Milt. What she saw was an F-27 with its skin off, stripped down with parts all over the floor.

"It looked like a Goodwill outlet for airplane parts," she remembers.

Then she met Milt Kuolt who was dressed in tight jeans and cowboy boots. He borrowed a nearby office for the interview and during the time he was talking with her, had one foot up on the desk. The interview was intimidating but she liked hearing his passion for people and his drive to serve. Maul became excited as Kuolt's philosophy was very much in line with hers.

Interview ended, Kuolt invited Maul to come see the airplane. Stepping inside the skeleton, there wasn't an awful lot to see. What Maul remembers most is being introduced to Kathy Anderson, later to become Milt's wife, whom she recalls as "just sparkling." *Finally! Someone who is sane!*

Kathy Anderson's airline experience was as a flight attendant with the Jet Set travel club, but when she had first met Milt Kuolt years earlier at Thousand Trails, she was really looking for a regular full time job where she could still fly weekends.

Kathy had a genuine sensitivity for the service end of the business. She screened and hired flight attendants with a perfectionist attitude and her sparkling personality.

Dee Dee Maul joined Horizon Air in May of 1981, knowing full well she had many daunting tasks to accomplish before the first flight in September; most of which Kuolt, with no previous airline experience, was completely unaware.

Just to confirm the work ahead, Maul asked Kuolt,

"Are we going to do any interline tariffs or do any work with the major carriers?"

"I don't know what you're talking about but, no, I don't think so. Just point to point will be all that we'll be doing."

"So you're going to be flying out of SeaTac?"

"Yes."

"Then you already have your lease agreements and gate space?"

"No, that's your job."

"Are you going to do interline ticketing?"

"Yeah, if we need to, I guess so."

"Then you already have your IATA number?"

"Whatever that is, if we need it, you get it. That's why we're bringing you on."

Normally a six-month time frame is required for the IATA four-letter designator, ticket counter and gate space. Maul walked away from the meeting thinking,

This guy Kuolt doesn't have a clue. He's just blowing smoke. We'll never be able to do it.

The task would have to be accomplished in *six* weeks.

"Our three-letter designator was 481," Maul recalls. "And we couldn't issue a ticket without that. QX was the two-letter designator that had to be combined with the 481." Maul went to Cufley and exclaimed,

"I can't believe none of this stuff has been done!"

Both of them then began working the problem. First, Dee Dee called the International Airline Transport Association (IATA) in Washington D.C. and told them she had to have the appropriate designator within 30 days. She received the typical bureaucratic response that it couldn't be done as such action takes six months to a year. Undaunted, Maul established a friendship with the lady in the IATA office. Sensing the critical time frame for Dee Dee and the new carrier, the IATA employee cut through layers of bureaucracy to quickly complete the task. Unheard of, but done.

An area of disagreement arose when Ned Laird was brought in as a consultant and firmly stated that there was no valid reason Horizon should be an interline carrier. His limited vision was such that he would tell Kuolt that all the airline had to do was serve point to point and just the three cities originally considered. And that Boeing Field would be just fine as a base – that there was no need to consider SeaTac. The conflict between Dee Dee and Laird escalated when she flat out stated that she wanted passengers to be able to interline. That meant that tickets and bags checked in Yakima or Pasco could be checked all the way, for example, to NYC, LAX or SFO. The differing viewpoints were not easily understood by Milt, so he would go round and round with each. Dee Dee won in the end but the result was that she and Laird were not on speaking terms.

Another of Milt's philosophies was: "Don't get so hung up on doing things right, get focused on the right thing!" Learning that in her first interview with Kuolt, Dee Dee knew that *the right thing to do* was interline ticketing and baggage transfer. She believes today that if the young airline hadn't done interlining, it would have folded before even starting. To her, interline baggage and ticketing agreements were essential as passengers did not want to have to recheck their baggage onto a major carrier upon arrival in Seattle. She was adamant that it was not a debatable issue.

Indeed, before Horizon could fly its first passenger, much more groundwork had to be laid. During the first meeting with Port of Seattle officials at SeaTac, Maul was flatly informed that there was no counter space, nor was there any gate space available. She was told, "There is *no way* you are going to be able to serve in and out of SeaTac.

Period." Hearing this from Maul, Kuolt went into orbit. Maul scheduled a second meeting with the Port and this time Kuolt went with her.

Again, he was wearing blue jeans, a maverick-style shirt and cowboy boots. Maul, who had been in the airline business more than a dozen years by then, was dressed in a business suit. Since her time of employment with the new airline was short, she was too embarrassed and intimidated to say anything to the Chief. Going into the meeting she sensed the half dozen Port of Seattle officials were looking at Kuolt and thinking *who is this guy?* Maul tried to schmooz the officials into understanding that Horizon was going to start flying in just three months and that gate space was absolutely essential. She reiterated the fact that Horizon already had its 2-letter designator, baggage tickets and all the rest, to which the officials responded that there was no space. And, in fact there was a two to three year waiting list. Kuolt kept interjecting comments such as, "What the hell does that mean?" "What we need to do is find space." and "You can't do that!"

The best the Port of Seattle officials offered was the suggestion that Horizon might see if another carrier would lease gate and ticket counter space to them. – or, have someone else handle them. Milt Kuolt had never been able to cut creatures of conformity any slack and the Port of Seattle executives were no exception. The icy meeting ended on a sour note.

Following the officials' suggestion was impossible for Horizon. The carrier wanted to establish an operation that would exemplify the highest standards. Milt wanted it that way, an airline built around the premise: "It's our privilege to serve you!" Those words were identified with everything about Horizon; including its training programs and timetables.

Maul returned to her office.

This is never going to work! She and McCaw had hit it off from the very beginning and she felt she could talk with him about the seemingly insurmountable problem. She told McCaw, "We just cannot take Kuolt back to SeaTac again!"

McCaw knew Oris Dunham of the Port of Seattle professionally and went with Maul to another meeting. Bruce told Dee Dee, "Let's see what we can do to get back into their good graces."

Bruce and Dee Dee were a very good and highly successful negotiating team. McCaw began by telling Dunham and his associates how important it was to have close-in proximity for the regional airline passenger, "We'll never park more than four planes on the ramp at a time." *In later years, the south side of C Concourse would be jammed full of Horizon aircraft with twenty or more planes on the ramp during peak periods, serving both the interline as well as the commuter passenger. Ten years later, daily flights would number into the 100s.*

The Port wanted to put Horizon on SeaTac's A Concourse and the airline wanted C. The officials then responded with some very useful information. They told the duo that Eastern Airlines was going through a downsizing, cutting their flights from 10-12 a day to possibly six. Eastern however, wasn't anxious to relinquish any space as the carrier was hopeful of overcoming their circumstances. McCaw and Maul were told to explore the possibilities with Eastern's station manager, Pete Amish.

Dee Dee describes Amish as "a fabulous guy." In subsequent meetings, an excellent relationship was established. An agreement was reached to lease gate and ticket counter space; and another agreement that allowed Eastern to perform ground support for Horizon aircraft. Partnering was the only option Horizon had to get into SeaTac and Eastern, at that time, was the venue. Milt knew a close-in gate was essential. He reasoned that long walks in concourses for short flights wouldn't work. Eastern had

Gate C-2 which was not being used to board or deplane passengers. It had no jetway and was mainly used to store ground equipment. Also, it was in a non-sterile area, meaning passengers did not have security screening. In 1981 that was allowable for intrastate travel on aircraft with less than 60 seats. And, instead of Horizon finding itself in the middle of nowhere, it was as close in as a passenger could get, less than 100 feet from the entrance to the terminal concourse.

Captain Mary Bardon, left, and First Officer, Monica Mygatt, (along with Flight Attendant Louise Van Dorn, not pictured) comprised Horizon's first all-female flight crew in July, 1984

The "Hands On" CEO

When Horizon first started, it had a manual system for reservations that literally involved index cards, sorted in bins on a large turntable. The reservationists sat around one large table. Each flight had its own bin for each day of the month. Computerized systems for Horizon were still some time out. Kuolt was known to walk into the reservations department, wanting to know, up to the minute, how each flight was booked. He demanded a high service response standard. No phone should ring more than twice. No one should be on hold for more than twenty seconds. He would stand there, taking the reservationist's time, trying to determine how many reservations had been booked and would be ecstatic if he learned any flights were full. He would inquire how many non-revenue passengers were on the flight. Originally, flights would often be loaded with family and friends of Horizon. That made the appearance of good load factors.

Maul recalls Pete Amish of Eastern was good to the Horizon staff. That part of the

(Courtesy Horizon Air Six Month Report to Stockholders, *March 31, 1984.)*

partnership began to work well until Kuolt made an unexpected appearance on a day when a Horizon flight was going to be delayed an hour and a half because a light was out in the F-27's baggage compartment. The Eastern maintenance people couldn't stop to change the light bulb because they were working their own L-1011 flight. Kuolt was a grinder for on-time departures. Most of the pilots knew that in Kuolt's mind, what constituted an on-time departure was the door was closed, the chocks were pulled, the engines were running and the wheels began to move one minute before scheduled departure. No matter what! His goal was educating Horizon passengers to understand that this airline's planes sometimes departed even *before* their scheduled time.

Kuolt was livid about the light bulb that had nothing to do with flight safety or anything else for that matter. He started yelling at Maul about the "damned light bulb."

"Milt, just cool it! We can't do anything about it because of our agreement with Eastern," Maul reminded him. And, Eastern's baggage handlers *would not* load the baggage because the light was out. Rules were rules and the union workers knew them well. Maul says that it wasn't that Milt didn't understand union rules, it was that he *chose not* to understand and decided they were irrelevant.

Milt's tension was building to a point that if it were electricity it could have powered the lights through four NFL quarters and an overtime. He watched the Eastern grunts lollygagging, moving at a pace that would have done a Tim Conway proud in the Carol Burnett TV shoe salesman skit.

Milt's circuits blew. He grabbed the light bulb, crawled up into the cargo bin and screwed the bulb in himself. Then, to the Eastern baggage guys, he yelled, "Now, load those damn bags!"

Maul was horrified. She moaned, "Oh, my God," knowing she was going to get a call from Pete Amish. She did. Although Pete admired the way Horizon innovated, he told Dee Dee, "You gotta do something, you gotta tell Milt we have union regulations!" Relaying the concern to Milt, she knew she would get a response to "tell them to go stuff it" or something stronger.

There were, however, a couple of Eastern crew chiefs on the ramp who really admired Milt for doing what they thought their executives might not have done. *Maybe that is another reason Horizon is where it is today and Eastern has gone into oblivion.*

Eastern had an employee lounge on ramp level complete with color television, microwave and stereo system. Their crew would be loafing around, making their microwave popcorn and watching replays of MASH on the tube while a Horizon plane was waiting for baggage to be loaded. One day, seeing this, Kuolt unloaded on them. He grabbed the popcorn, shut off the television set and yelled like a banshee. The men didn't know what to think but they hopped to it. Kuolt gave something back to them by teaching them a better work ethic. Milt Kuolt always walks a fine line between really upsetting people and gaining incredible respect from them.

Small incidents continued to happen. There was a gate employee who irritated Kuolt for whatever reason. Kuolt would yell at him and he would cry. Then Kuolt would get even more upset that the guy would cry because he felt that every person should be mature enough to accept responsibility and expect criticism.

Dee Dee Maul remembers another especially memorable incident when Kuolt was helping out at the gate. He was dressed in blue jeans, a short-sleeved shirt and a cowboy hat. And he was smoking a cigarette. *This was before smoking was prohibited on concourses and in the terminal.* Kuolt was tagging bags when one of the gate attendants said softly to Maul, "You know, Dee Dee, he's smoking behind the counter."

Kuolt had ground Maul mercilessly about her people and how they performed so she figured, *It's my turn!* She checked out just what Kuolt had been doing and where. Later, she walked into Kuolt's office.

"I need a few minutes of your time, Milt. I want you to know I appreciate the help when we're busy but the next time you are at the gate, I ask that you be dressed appropriately and no smoking beyond the gate. If you are willing to go out there without the Matt Dillon getup, that's fine." And she left.

Kuolt was incredulous. He immediately phoned McCaw.

"You're not going to believe this! You are not going to believe this! I just got ground on by Maul! She was right on!"

It was as if it was the first time anyone had ever backed him against the wall.

Milt Kuolt is a CEO for whom no task is too menial. Besides helping where he perceived assistance was needed, he would frequently show up in the early morning hours with donuts for ramp and counter personnel.

He was not above helping elsewhere such as dumping the honey buckets from the F-27's lavatories which didn't have holding tanks that could be pumped out, such as are found on newer aircraft. He would put the bucket on a truck and take it where it could be dumped at the other end of the field. *If the president of United or American Airlines had done that, it would have made the six o'clock news nationally.*

Milt's work ethic permeated the organization. It wasn't unusual to see flight attendants helping clean the inside of the airplane or pilots on the outside washing an F-27 before the next day's operation.

Along with the strong work ethic, Horizon was becoming recognized as the airline with class. And professionals, other than employees, made their distinct contributions. Sheila Hardwick was contracted to handle catering and uniforms, working closely with Dee Dee and Kathy Anderson. Sheila developed supporting materials and concepts that would fit in with the color scheme of the red sun on the Horizon logo developed by Bill Lloyd. Sheila went to a Bellevue boutique where the items were good but very, very pricey. Maul remembers the cost of pilot uniforms was initially $800 each and flight attendant uniforms were about $500. She is certain that Kuolt was unaware of the costs until much later.

"Everything was first class. Our flight attendants had burgundy Coach handbags and suitcases. There was not another regional carrier that could match Horizon's class. Which, I believe, was one of the key reasons we were able to compete the way we did."

Dee Dee Maul and Bruce McCaw were the team that got things done. Veterans will remember the Navy's Seabee's during World War II who were identified with "the difficult we do immediately – the impossible takes a little longer." That was McCaw and Maul. Dee Dee would tell Bruce what was needed, tell him who the people were, and they would attack the problem. And, it worked. She knew the lay of the land, and McCaw could go in with advance knowledge of a particular situation.

A particular sticky situation arose with the airport manager at Pasco. His name was Paul Vic and he had been an airport consultant at Paine Field when McCaw was on the Airport Advisory Commission and involved there with JetAir. When McCaw saw Vic's name, he told Maul, "I can work with this guy. He and I have a great relationship and mutual respect." And the deal was negotiated. The same magic worked in Eugene, Oregon where a former college buddy of McCaw's was involved. Other airlines didn't want Horizon to compete in the Oregon city. But McCaw and Maul got it done.

The Media

The September 1, 1981 Horizon inaugural flight from Seattle to Yakima caught a lot of attention from the media and the general public. One week later, service was inaugurated to Pasco in the Tri-Cities.

Radio announcers have this problem on their first day of new employment. They give the call letters of the last radio station. On the inaugural Horizon flight to Yakima, an embarrassed Cufley greeted passengers with "Welcome to Cascade Flight 100!"

During this introduction to a new city, something happened which could have spelled the demise of the airline.

Just like the Yakima flight one week earlier, media was on board including a television news team from Seattle and representatives from the newspapers. As the aircraft began its approach over Hanford, the cockpit crew got a gearbox "LOW OIL PRESSURE!" warning light for the port engine. McRae, who was in the right seat, yelled at Cufley, "Do we shut it down and come in on one engine?" Mulling over the potential for negative press, Cufley responded, "No. For sure we would make the six o'clock news and if that happens, we may wind down this whole operation before we can crank it up!" So, with the warning light insistently bleating red into the cockpit, power was reduced for the one engine to take stress off the gearbox until touchdown.

Other often minor incidents took place in the operation of the F-27s. For example, a recurring false "FIRE WARNING!" light would appear. It could not be ignored and the F-27 had to either return to base or land at the closest possible airport until the cockpit team could be assured there was no fire.

Although a very good airplane, one of the problems with the F-27s was that Fairchild had stopped building them. It was now a much different company, not providing manufacturer support. Thus, after-market parts and technical support vendors had to be relied upon. Nevertheless, Horizon's maintenance team performed their tasks well, despite the circumstances. Horizon aggressively updated many of the systems and equipment on the F-27, making it a much better and more reliable aircraft.

The fire warning system, for instance, was not of recent vintage and its thermal covers were subject to cracking, creating frequent false warnings.

Another time, when an F-27 was flying into Medford from Portland, the plane had iced up and its deicers could not cope with the build up. Even with full power, its designated altitude could not be maintained. It was in a constant rate of descent. Finally touching down safely at its destination, ice was still clinging to the leading edge of the wings. Despite occasional inconveniences, the F-27 was still regarded as a very good airplane for Pacific Northwest passenger service. This single deicing problem was an exception.

Horizon F-27 welcomed in Yakima, the first city served.

On -Time Departures

At Horizon Air, everyone was committed to the vision. Everyone pulled on the same end of the rope to make things happen.

Tom Cufley remembers one of his first meetings with Milt was his introduction to *A Message To Garcia*. "What it amounted to was you don't ask a lot of dumb questions. You identify your mission and you go out and complete it."

Dee Dee Maul recalls, "I remember Milt would know the first thing in the morning if there was a flight delay of any kind." Cufley adds, "It was either you or me that was on the line for that. If it was either a mechanical problem or a pilot who wasn't on board on time, we had better have the right answers." So either Maul or Cufley was always prepared for that early morning phone call and there had to be a very good reason why a flight was late.

Early on, Horizon's flights were out of SeaTac and maintenance was out of Boeing Field. This presented some very challenging moments. One particular evening a flight was going to be delayed because of a mechanical problem. Alan Zanouzoski, Captain on the flight, said to Maul, "You know, we got the part we need at the Boeing Field hangar. If we can get it, we still are out on time."

So Alan and Dee Dee jumped into her RX-7 and "drove 85 miles an hour from SeaTac to Boeing," feverishly hoping to get there before the facility locked up. With heavy traffic, they arrived a couple of minutes after all of Dick Heaton's mechanics had left for the day. Alan tried to jimmy the lock but couldn't.

"What'll we do, Alan?" Dee Dee was desperate.

"We'll have to break the damn lock!" the pilot retorted.

"With what?"

"See that fire extinguisher? It looks heavy enough to do the job." Alan grabbed the extinguisher from its mount on the outside of the building. The only thing on his mind at the moment was getting the necessary part. He would deal with any fallout later. Jamming the fire extinguisher through the chain, he gained entrance to the maintenance hangar. The pair raced up and down the aisles, searching scores of parts bins. Alan finally found the right bin and scooped up the part. The valiant duo raced back to SeaTac, found the Eastern Airlines support guys who installed it and the flight departed on time.

Well, Maul's resourcefulness didn't earn her any plaudits from Kuolt, who raked her. She also received the wrath of maintenance chief Heaton the next morning. His concern was the unsecured facility with a million dollars worth of parts. Maul told Heaton, "If you would get the damn airplanes over to SeaTac in the morning, I would get them out on time!" The pair went back and forth on the issue until Kuolt had to get right in the middle of it. Fifteen years later, Heaton is still miffed about the incident. Although Maul and Heaton had their differences, they worked together with mutual respect and developed a deep friendship.

Maul said later that Horizon coined a phrase, "We'd break down doors for an on-time departure," which is exactly what they had done. In Maul's opinion, "Perceptions were much different in maintenance. They could never quite understand why we were so driven to achieve high on-time ratings. Maintenance, not being on site, couldn't comprehend the pressure we experienced from Milt for on-time departures."

Not wanting to break into any more hangars for an on-time departure, Maul started showing up at the Boeing maintenance hangar early in the morning to ensure that the planes would get off the field in time and to SeaTac for scheduled 7:00 a.m. departures. She tried to sweet-talk Heaton into urging his team to get the planes moving. Hanging around one morning, Maul stumbled upon one of Heaton's mechanics who lived out of his boat which was parked alongside the hangar. The individual was taking a shower under the hazardous chemical rinse. "Well," Maul trundled off, "I guess a guy's got to maintain his personal hygiene."

Another "on-time departure" confrontation took place between Heaton and Kuolt after maintenance had moved to Portland following the Air Oregon acquisition. The flap revolved around a flight scheduled for take off soon on a route different from its usual schedule. A frustrated Heaton called Kuolt in Seattle, "Milt, I don't think we are going to make it. This airplane just isn't cooperating!" It was undergoing a major refurbishing and had been added to the schedule assuming completion.

Kuolt retorted, "Get on your people! Don't just talk to them!"

On the last day before the scheduled departure, Heaton knew there was no way the plane would be ready. He called Seattle and, unable to reach Kuolt, told someone else to relay the message. Kuolt called back a few minutes later. Heaton went back upstairs from the hangar floor and he recalls Kuolt started working him over. "He just chewed and chewed and chewed," Heaton told others later, until he had had enough.

"No, I'll tell *you*, Mr. Kuolt!"

Kuolt shot back, "Well, I got some options and I guess I had better exercise them."

"Well, you had better damn well start exercising them," Heaton yelled, "because I damn well want to tell you something! You don't know a damned thing about what's going on down here. If you had any idea about what the hell is going on, you wouldn't be wasting my damned time running back and forth answering the friggin' phone which ain't going to do you any good anyway!" Heaton abruptly hung up the phone, which by now was too hot to touch.

Kuolt took the next flight to Portland and appeared in the maintenance hangar about 45 minutes after the phone call. He walked up to Heaton and said,

"Father Heaton, are you still pissed at me?"

"Hell, no!" was the reply.

Ken Hobby joined Horizon in 1984, brought in by Dick Heaton to replace Stan Anderson who was "V-P-maintenance." Dick, who had been aboard since day one, was an old friend of Ken's when both were at the old Hughes Air West, later Republic and then were at United. Ken's initial title was the director of maintenance

Kenneth L. Hobby

and when Anderson left, he became "V-P-maintenance."

Ken reflects today, "One of the things that was so great about Horizon was a whole different perspective on maintenance. Many who maintain the large aircraft for major airlines think that the task would be much less with a regional carrier with smaller aircraft. Such was not the case." Ken retired from Horizon at the beginning of 2000, saying "It was a great sixteen years."

Going First Class

I t had to give Cascade Airways' management heartburn to learn that an F-27 with 40 seats was leaving with a full load while their Beech 99s, with 13 seats, were flying half empty. Other comparisons were only too obvious. Flight attendants, food, drinks, a pressurized aircraft with a lavatory ... the Beech 99s had none of those frills. Horizon's top quality flight attendant uniforms and complimentary Coach bags at the beginning may have seemed like a bit of an overkill. Those concerns were put to rest about a week after Horizon began flying when a United ticket counter agent came up to Dee Dee Maul, saying, "I have never seen an airline with so much class!" To have another airline's employee notice their touch of class helped build a lot of pride in Horizon's people.

Horizon had a Bellevue catering firm deliver croissants and strawberries hand-dipped in chocolate. To be sure, everyone who experienced Horizon's efforts at superior service, was quick to pass on this information to other potential passengers as well. Keep in mind the average flight was only 50 minutes long.

Nothing Horizon did was traditional commuter airline style. Although the F-27s were not new, off-the-assembly-line aircraft, the one million dollars plus spent to refurbish each aircraft was a sound investment. The planes had brand new paint jobs with excellently designed interiors, new seats and upgraded avionics.

"I remember the Cascade gumshoes snooping around the ramp personnel at Horizon," Cufley laughs. "One day a Cascade informer asked one of our employees what his job was. Suspecting the individual was from the competing carrier, he curtly replied, 'We make horses' heads and send them to Spokane for completion.'"

Sales and Marketing

As time went on, Eastern was losing money faster than it could be printed and their people were demoralized. Horizon's cheery, efficient staff was a breath of fresh air to them and some fine relationships were forged over time between Horizon and Eastern personnel.

Don Welsh was just 22 and working for United Airlines when he got the call from Nane Aluli who was director of sales and marketing for another airline, telling him about a new airline, Horizon. Although Joe Clark initially offered Aluli the job at Horizon, he had declined but suggested Joe contact "this high energy young guy, Don Welsh." Besides, Clark was told, "Welsh won't cost you much." *Those were two of the attributes that would gain almost anyone an interview at the new carrier.*

Welsh was another whose introduction to Horizon was a meeting with Joe Clark at the old Boeing Field hangar. Don passed muster with Joe who suggested that Welsh prepare a sales and marketing plan as to "how you would market this airline." Being

Don Welsh

a young guy just out of school and filled with unbounded confidence, Welsh crafted what he believed was needed to get the airline recognized and to generate revenues. Clark reviewed the plan. "Well," he told the aspiring young man, "you are going to get a chance to meet Milt Kuolt and present your plan to him."

Welsh had heard about Milt Kuolt. His first meeting was in Kuolt's offices at Thousand Trails. He remembers Kuolt's appearance as intimidating. The Chief was wearing jeans with a big belt buckle and a shirt open at the collar. The meeting was scheduled for late afternoon so it wasn't long after it began that it was, as usual, cocktail time for Milt. Therefore the review of Welsh's sales and marketing plan actually took place later that evening. A day or two thereafter, Welsh heard from Clark that the position was his.

Welsh viewed it as a great opportunity. He thought, *This is going to be pretty wild. You have this playboy type, Joe Clark, along with Kuolt, who is a combination of a Howard Hughes and Ted Turner.* Welsh, however, had no doubt Horizon would be a success. The vision and commitment articulated by Joe and Milt was so clear that he believed there was no room for failure.

Coming on board, Welsh knew that the airline absolutely had to deliver on the promise that it was going to provide a high level of service on short haul flights. From a sales standpoint, travel agencies all over Eastern Washington had to be convinced that Horizon was for real and that the carrier was well capitalized so it could handle both the good days and the bad.

"It's funny now," Welsh sighs, "I'm 43 and that was nearly twenty years ago. At the time, we really worked hard to get the task accomplished. Of all the things I've done in my career, I am most proud of my association with Horizon."

The association included a number of marketing challenges, especially when the young airline was having its first cash flow crunch. Welsh initiated the prepaid ticket booklet concept, a plan to get cash on the front end from Eastern Washington travel agents who could then resell the booklets to their clients who were frequent fliers to Seattle. Welsh's salesmanship was especially evident during one particularly tough low-cash period. He was out of the office all of one week, personally collecting checks in advance sales of ticket books from Yakima and Pasco travel agents and, when he returned that Friday, he brought back $70,000. That was a major part of payroll. Welsh says that if it hadn't been for the support of the travel agents, he believes the airline would have had a much tougher time. Maybe even folded.

Sure it was a scheme to collect cash up front but it worked so well that the plan was recycled a couple more times after its initial success with Welsh convincing the agents of the excellent value they were getting.

John Kuolt, who was "V-P," marketing and Milt's brother, remembers well how aggressive Horizon was in acquainting communities with the airline. He recalls how teams were formed to go into a new city such as Eugene, Springfield, or Bend-Redmond, with a couple of pilots, two flight attendants, and sales people including himself, Don Welsh and/or Mark Bocci.

"We would go into every business in that city and hand out packets of information on Horizon," John reflects today.

"We also had fists full of ball point pens with our logo and Horizon schedules. We would talk to anyone who would listen to how we were entering the market and how we could significantly improve their travel.

"Later, when we had code sharing with United Airlines, we had an arrangement where United would pay 80 percent or more of an evening get together for travel agents. We would outline the combined service that both United and Horizon will offer the community to any destination in the world." *Perhaps the only benefit from code sharing – more on that later.*

One point in particular helped Horizon "turn the corner" in the Yakima Valley and Tri Cities area when McDonald's fast food outlets did a joint promotion with Horizon. It was viewed as most unusual when Horizon was on all meal placemats for six weeks. "There were thousands of them. And, we had a cartoon of Horizon that kids would color and sign," John recalls. "They would send it in and vie for a free round trip on Horizon with their parents. It was a very big promotion and we got a lot of attention from other airlines as ours was the little carrier that was able to get this major tie in."

Persistent in their enterprising ways, Horizon's marketing people came up with a small package express service called "SunStreak." It was a counter-to-counter flat rate opportunity to rapidly move single shipments weighing 50 pounds or less. Parcels could be dropped off a half-hour before a scheduled departure and shipped to any Horizon destination, initially for only $25. "Sunair" was another innovative idea by the carrier, providing regular as well as priority airfreight service.

Shortly after its September 1, 1981 inaugural flight, the carrier began flying cargo along with passengers. They moved everything from gold bullion to a tiger. *Bet you thought flying tigers was someone else's business.* But Horizon did just that in 1984 when it flew an eight-month-old tiger cub from Coos Bay, Oregon to Portland. Baby seals and chickens were some of the other more unusual items in the cargo compartment.

Tight security revolved around the gold shipments that were accompanied by a guard. The gold was off-loaded into an armored vehicle. It was not unusual for air cargo weight to "gross out" between such points as Portland to Boise, Portland to Medford and Seattle to Boise. Direct sales promotion by the three-person team included John Kuolt, Bill Ayer and Don Welsh. They covered all cities served by Horizon and were credited with significantly boosting air cargo revenues.

By 1985, this segment of the business exceeded forecasts for every month of the year. At year-end, over $3.4 million in air cargo revenues were logged, up 72 percent over the previous year. Air cargo contributed to much greater profit margins than air passenger mile revenues. Bob Oakley was director of freight. In focusing on this service in addition to serving passengers, Horizon Air was able to accelerate to become Number Two nationally in regional airline freight volumes; second only to Air Wisconsin.

Early flight crews, mechanics, and executives.

Market Share

S cheduling strategy was another factor that allowed Horizon to successfully compete with Republic and Cascade Airways. First, Horizon had the aircraft, both the 19-seat Metroliner, (with the acquisition of Air Oregon) and the 40-passenger, pressurized F-27. The versatility of aircraft allowed for scheduling to a particular market. Early market analysis confirmed the need for equipment big enough to feel like an airplane and small enough to provide a frequency of at least three flights a day. The F-27s, the Metroliner IIs, and later, Metroliner IIIs, made Horizon a formidable competitor with other airlines *and the passenger car.*

Yes, indeed! In markets such as Wenatchee, Washington and Redmond, Oregon, there was a time when passengers had such a long wait between flights, they could get to

Seattle or Portland more quickly behind the wheel. Horizon remedied that with its perceptive marketing strategy and frequency of flights.

Frequent flyers experienced Horizon's pressurized aircraft, with flight attendants, food and beverage service and lavatories, none of which Cascade had offered them. And there was that unmistakable commitment to service, Milt Kuolt's credo.

They loved it.

Soon passengers began to automatically book Horizon. Many business travelers, such as those with Battelle Northwest in Richland, began requesting their in-house travel managers choose only Horizon. Schedules and more destination cities were added to accommodate the increased demand.

One of the most innovative things Horizon did was the "carry your baggage to the plane, load it on the cart and pick it up as you deplane," says Mel Kays, Horizon's former CFO.

"I believe that way of baggage handling was invented by Horizon and now all the regional carriers do it. One of the cute stories about this method of handling baggage is the one about the sweet little old lady who carried her bag out to the plane at SeaTac, put it on the cart and boarded the plane. Now, all of the baggage carts look pretty much the same, both at origin and destination.

When arriving at the destination, the little old lady deplaned and was amazed to see her luggage sitting on the same cart she had placed it on at SeaTac. When she asked one of the pilots how the cart got there so fast, he replied, 'We just hooked it to the tail and flew!'"

Welsh remembers Kuolt delivering extra measures of appreciation to the crews who were working so hard to make his dream come true. It was never a surprise to Welsh and others to spot Milt at various stations at five or six in the morning. He was cleaning lavatories, bringing in donuts for baggage handlers, the pilots and dispatchers and otherwise quietly helping out. Welsh said, "There are so many good memories, it would be difficult to recount them all. Like when we went into Medford, Oregon and saw the acceptance the community gave us. Milt had surrounded himself with an eclectic group of personalities. I look back at people like Scott Kidwell and Ned Laird, a consultant to Horizon. Kuolt was so skilled at assembling a diverse group, each person different from him and giving him counsel. The older I get, the more I realize how important that was. It enabled him to assimilate their knowledge like a computer and then to kick out the right answers."

Pat "Zack" Zachwieja joined Horizon in the first few months of operation as Manager of Flight Dispatch. He remembers his greatest concern at the time was whether he would have a job the next month. He attributes the carrier's on time performance in the early times as a credit to "all employees pulling together." He was transferred to Portland with the Air Oregon acquisition and today is "V-P," marketing and planning for Horizon.

William Ayer, now president of Alaska Airlines, was director of scheduling and planning for Horizon. "We were hell-bent on generating revenues and developing market share," he remembers. "That was the name of the game for the first three-plus years. I am not saying that was wrong. We had a specific window with Deregulation in 1978 and we had to move quickly or someone else would ace us out. So we jumped when we could and figured out what we were doing later."

Ayer and John Cox would evaluate new routes and felt pressure for Horizon to stay one move ahead of Cascade Airways. "You had to keep moving or they'd gain on you. It was a game. An important game," Ayer recalls.

It was quickly apparent that Horizon had to keep adding new city pairs to maintain its dominance in the marketplace. Cascade had been getting a government subsidy to provide one-a-day flights into Wenatchee. A market analysis suggested that there was greater potential there. The automobile was the primary competition in serving the Central Washington city.

Kuolt's sales and marketing team huddled and it was determined that Horizon could serve Wenatchee without a subsidy. Cascade, which would have lost money without it, publicly scoffed. Nevertheless, Horizon went in on September 9, 1984 and demonstrated to the public the advantages of flying to Seattle over driving and was almost immediately profitable.

"Depending on a subsidy, such as Cascade Airways did, was no encouragement to improve service," Bill Ayer says. "We viewed Wenatchee as a very viable marketplace and it has been proven many times over. Today, in the year 2001, Horizon provides seven round trips daily with Dash 8 service.

"Milt Kuolt was a true visionary in the post-deregulation period," Ayer reflects. "Horizon pioneered the model."

Horizon was moving all right – through birth pains. When Kuolt was in the throes of uncertainty or concern about something, everyone within reach was affected. Many of the staff remember, for example, in the early days of the airline, the euphoria that would erupt when challenges were met head on and surmounted. This happened on a daily basis. These successes were celebrated in the late afternoon with rum and cokes, booze and pizza.

When former Cascade Airways employees Cufley and Maul both signed on with Horizon, it caused no small stir back in Spokane. The word was that there was some outfit in Seattle that they had taken up with. They thought it was called HORIZON. So some of Cascade's last-gasp employees derisively dubbed the new operation "artificial horizon," which of course, is a part of the instrument panel on an aircraft. Horizon employees just smiled.

Milt admits that the airline had a "strategy" but really had no master plan. "You know, I was so gullible that when someone would say, 'Milt, you gotta come into Pullman, or you have to come into some city in Oregon,' I'd say, 'yeah, we'll do that,' never giving it much thought. I figured that if the community wanted it then we would go in. I didn't go through all the analysis. I think that motivated some of those who believed in us. We learned the hard way that some of those cities could not support the size of aircraft, with the frequency we wanted to operate, using two 40-passenger and one 19-passenger airplanes. Reflecting back today, I would have handled some of the destinations differently. A long-range master plan would have helped immensely and kept us from making mistakes. Yeah, we were a wild bunch – a real wild bunch."

Show Me The Money – Bankers and Lending

I n the early days of Horizon Air's growth, Milt Kuolt would say, "The way to make a small fortune in the airline business is to start with a big one." He discovered that there are bankers of every stripe to help you along like the Seafirst bankers of the 1970s who were suckered by frauds and fakers selling Oklahoma oil deals and others who would redline areas where they wouldn't go with any kind of deal. Kuolt had met them all and said, "There's nothing worse than a nervous banker." In a story for Washington CEO magazine over a decade ago, Milt characterized commercial bankers thusly:

"Typically they have access to large amounts of capital but usually are ill-prepared to understand the risks involved with a venture. They focus too much on the product or technology and often fail to accurately assess the integrity or nature of the individual; and they seem to be taken in by every smooth talking dude that walks through their doors."

Of course, with the advent of the Internet and e-commerce high flyers in the late 1990s, it was the venture capitalists who rewrote the book.

Then there were the investment bankers.

As the CEO of Thousand Trails, Milt not only had to sell campground memberships, he had to sell bankers on backing the enterprise. "It wasn't *tough* to sell the banks," Kuolt recalls. "It was damn near impossible." The only bank that would touch the deal was Canadian Imperial but it would only advance $90,000 against $200,000 in receivables. Kuolt remembers the experience taught him some hard lessons about entrepreneurship.

"I recognized that entrepreneurs shouldn't really talk with bankers. They should work through an intermediary."

Commercial banking regulations have forever left their imprint on Kuolt. He cites an experience when he had deposited $5 million in a Seattle bank and a couple of weeks later was notified that because of this great collateral, he could borrow $3 million more. Kuolt was incensed.

There was one certain banker from whom Kuolt had sought a business loan only to be turned down. Not one to mince words, Milt told the banker what he thought of his decision-making ability and also where *he* could deposit *his* money.

Fast forward a few years to Horizon Air. Kuolt contacted David Sawyer who had years earlier put together various financings for Thousand Trails.

"Sawyer, we're losing a fair amount of money and I was wondering if you could take a look at things and help us out?"

"How much are you losing? Sawyer wanted to know.

"About five hundred thousand a month."

"For how long?"

"Too friggin' long! We gotta find a way to cut these losses."

Sawyer knew that Kuolt always ran things tight anyway but said he would return to the mainland from Hawaii and take a look at the operation.

Sawyer looked in all the drawers, in all the cubbyholes and in all the books. He concluded the carrier was losing even more than Kuolt knew.

"Milt, I'm going to lay it right on the line," Sawyer warned Horizon's CEO. "You had better have an awful lot of assets because you're going to have to sell them all. Things don't look good anytime in the foreseeable future."

Kuolt countered, "So what are your thoughts?"

The answer came in a somber tone: "I really have none."

"Well, can you stick around and work with us a bit?" Kuolt asked, knowing he didn't have the money to pay Sawyer either. His old friend agreed to do what he could and set about task number one: finding financing. It would require the sale of many of Kuolt's personal assets and likely the mortgaging of anything else of value.

Horizon's primary money concerns were financing of aircraft and additional financing for operations. Sawyer was greeted with a hearty laugh from bankers and others who found no merit in his proposal. Sawyer investigated the "mouse houses," a term coined to describe alternative financing sources. Kuolt thought the interest rates they demanded could be characterized as extortion. He managed to avoid their enticements and walk away.

"We had sold a lot of Milt's personal things, including a sizable investment in gold," Sawyer remembered. "We were running out of time and unsure what to do next. Then a little magic happened. We were together in one of the many finance meetings that typically ended with drinks to ease the pain, when there was a knock on the door. The gentleman introduced himself as a director with Air Oregon and he said simply, 'Would you like to buy an airline?'"

It was Bob Booth, one of the founders and chairman of Air Oregon. This wasn't the first overture from Air Oregon. Milt had received earlier calls from both Don Streun, Air Oregon's president and from another board member, Andy Andersen.

After Booth's question, *"Would you like to buy an airline?"* there was a moment of silence, followed by exchanged glances.

"Then we all laughed out loud," Sawyer said. Kuolt's smile disappeared instantly. "We don't have any money!" He blurted out just how bleak the situation was. Still, Booth, Kuolt and the others started talking together and set another meeting to talk some more.

Sawyer had mined the investment community, leaving no stone unturned. On an earlier occasion he was able to arrange a meeting with a Spokane bank to try yet another source of financing for Horizon. Sawyer had a commitment letter for $2 million and the bank asked to meet the Horizon CEO in person to firm it up. "Milt, this looks good. I have rubber stamp approval for this," Sawyer assured him.

"Well, just who is this person that is going to issue this 'rubber stamp'?" Kuolt demanded.

"I don't know the individual," Sawyer responded quickly, "but I do know there will be no problem."

Sawyer called the bank back to set the meeting and casually asked who would be signing off on the loan. Sawyer gave Kuolt the name the next day as they were about to leave for the bank. Kuolt was uncharacteristically quiet.

"Listen, I don't want to burst your balloon," he said softly, "but we're going to end up with an empty sack."

"Why?"

"I don't know. We'll go to the meeting but I don't think it's going to go through."

On arrival at the bank, the person who had been so positive with Sawyer that the deal was workable, entered the room stammering and stuttering, obviously at a loss for words to describe his point of view. Finally, he nearly shouted out, "We can't do this deal. I can't meet with you. We can't do this!"

Apparently, bankers have long memories. This happened to be the same banker Kuolt had agitated years earlier when seeking financing for Thousand Trails.

Other bankers who were longer on vision and shorter on memory, however, had backed Thousand Trails to its current success.

Milt Kuolt, skillful negotiator, stepped forward, not so much seeking a middle ground with the banker, but letting others believe that his stated position *was* the middle ground. Dismissing the frustrated banker's decision, Kuolt asked what they were going to charge for financing. This was of primary importance in an era of very high interest rates. When he heard the figure, Kuolt said resolutely, "I was thinking more like two percent." The way Milt said "two percent," Sawyer believed he really meant two percent.

"I don't think banks have made two percent loans since Alexander Hamilton was Secretary of the Treasury," offered a surprised Sawyer. But Kuolt was making a point. He would not move from that figure. Sawyer wanted this bank loan so he joined in the discussion of the rate and, because Milt held on so firmly to the "two percent," negotiations settled back down to a businesslike discussion of the possibilities and they were able to shave a half point from the original figure. The fact that Horizon was providing a valuable air service to their cities put additional pressure on the bankers and a deal was struck.

Perhaps the most challenging time was about a year and half after startup when Horizon was trying to build its fleet and was on the hook with lenders for millions of dollars. At the time, Horizon had moved all of its accounts from Peoples Bank in Seattle to US Bank in Oregon. By then, Sawyer's role with the carrier had diminished but he was still providing occasional consultation.

"Horizon had been missing payments on its planes and the consortium of banks wanted to take the airplanes back and shut the company down," Sawyer recalled. "So, they sent their top loan officers to give Milt the news. When they showed up at Horizon, Milt acted like he didn't know why they were there."

After a few introductory comments, the bankers came right to the point, saying, "We can't deal with the missed installments and want to know what you are going to do about it." There was a momentary silence. Kuolt rose from his chair, looked around the room, then directly into the bankers' faces. Throwing his keys on the table, he shouted, "You want the planes? Here are the keys. Go fly all of them to wherever you want to. If not, I'll fly them into your office!"

The bankers exchanged startled looks. Sawyer recalled years later that he thought they actually believed Kuolt would do just that.

Mike Lowry, who was Horizon's "V-P," finance, then ripped into the banker, reminding him that for a loan of perhaps two million dollars, and based upon the agreement with another aircraft manufacturer, the bank had collateral of seven to nine million dollars.

The banker then backed off some, but still the relationship was strained as the bank was threatening yet to call the loan. *For the most part, Horizon never really had clear sailing with its banks until the airline was sold.*

The meeting abruptly adjourned. The bankers never again called about repossessing the planes, making payments or anything. Sawyer said later, "It was kind of like a loan extension without words. I've never seen anything quite like it. After the bankers had gone, Kuolt said something to me like: 'I guess I'll have to learn how to fly.'"

For a very long period, Horizon struggled for ways to finance its aircraft acquisitions. It was a constant cycle of moving from one bank to another because the existing bank was so jittery. There seemed no way to eliminate the unabated losses.

A Talk Given to the Investment Banking Community

San Francisco, October 24, 1984

By Milt Kuolt, President, Horizon Air

We started Horizon Air three years ago, in September 1981. At that point, we had two airplanes, today we have 30. When we started, we had 60 employees, today we have 900. We had three cities when we started, today we serve 22. The first month, we carried 800 passengers and this month we carried 75,000. Let me cover the three basic reasons for starting Horizon Air:

I left Thousand Trails and was looking for a new challenge.

I enjoy the service business and also the embryonic or start-up stage of a company. $100-$150 million in sales – 1,500 employees is the range in which

I like to work and work best.

Third, a good friend, Joe Clark, said there was a real void in the Northwest for a good service-oriented regional airline, one that effectively covered the territory of Oregon, Idaho and Washington state, plus maybe a little more.

Goals

We have just one goal; one that we set when we started Horizon and that is to be <u>the best regional airline in the country.</u> When I say "the best," I mean from three points of view and in the following order of importance:

from the view of the employee: I want the employee to believe that this is the best regional airline that they can work for;

from the view of the customer: we want them to feel that Horizon is the best airline they have ever flown, where the passenger can be dealt with honestly and expect excellence and lastly:

from the view of the investor: I want us to be the most profitable regional airline in the country.

Being the largest airline has never been Horizon's goal. Expansion for expansion's sake has never been part of the plan. We have expanded, but I can promise that it was the result of opportunities that presented themselves. As you should know, when you are the best, it's real easy to get bigger. You in the investment business ought to know that because it's damn tough to be the best when you're the biggest. While I may not rate ourselves today to be the best regional airline in the country, even though I'm tempted to, that does continue to be our goal. Nearly all of our employees are non-union. Up until now I don't believe our employees have felt a need for union representation. I believe we have excellent employee-management relationships even with 900 employees. It's always tougher the bigger you get. There again, it's tough to be the best and have the best employer-employee relationships when you're that size.

Thoughts on Employees

We do a lot of work on technical training and human development. Horizon has a program titled "Investment in Excellence" that's optional for employees to attend although the majority of our employees have taken the course on their own time. It deals with self improvement and human development. You may hear many companies saying, "We've got to make better employees out of our people." Our feeling is that we want and need to make "better people out of our employees" – to build their self-esteem and make them feel good about what they're doing. This approach seems to work well.

We really get our people to achieve greater potential. All of you have heard the comment, "If only I had the money. If I just had the money, I could do this or invest in that." Well, if I had a choice, I'd take a checkbook of people over a checkbook full of money. I know that when I've got the right people working as a team, I'm able to get all the necessary financial support for the Company from investment bankers and reach our goals.

If we could clone the 900 people we have, we could double the size of our Company. And if we could clone it twice, we could have an airline that covers the entire region west of the Rockies. Now, that's what people can do and are all about. Those of you who manage people will know what I'm talking about. That's where the real assets of the Company are.

Rarely has money really been an overriding concern of mine. When I started Thousand Trails, I was virtually bankrupt for five years before we turned that Company around with a great team of people. When you don't have the financial resources, it's always a big concern. When you gain a little financial strength, you have to get off the money kick and work on the development of people within the organization. In any event, leadership is a hell of a lot more important than management.

The Customer

In our Company, the customer is always right – even when we know he is "off-base." In the mindset of our people, that customer is correct and that's the way we treat them. At least, that's the way I expect us to treat them. The airline industry as a whole has done a hell of a job training the public. They have trained the customer to expect mediocrity. Long lines, indifferent, rude and uncaring employees. Many behave like robots. Lost bags are the norm. In-flight service depends on the mood of the flight attendant. We want our customer on Horizon to expect excellence, not mediocrity. If the customer expects excellence, there's a hell of a better chance we will deliver excellence.

Management

The development of management in a fast-growth company is probably the most difficult task. So much depends on the first line supervisor to senior management. There is no truer statement than "The speed of the chief is the speed of the crew." Finding the talent is difficult because what I look for are the leadership instincts in the individual. I believe it is difficult to train people to be managers who don't have the natural instincts of leadership. I also stress that the managers in our organization are really the "water boys," cheerleaders and coaches to the people that report to them. They are there to help and serve the organization, not to be served or adored by their subordinates.

When I look at management, I look for integrity – that is my #1 requirement in Horizon or anything I'm involved in – self-discipline, good judgment and technical smarts. Behind that you have some interrelated things such as leadership, interpersonal skills, administration and planning. Integrity rates the highest and that's what I look for. I try to determine the degree of integrity of an individual.

Deregulation

If deregulation had been really in full force, I would not have had the appetite to get into this business. We are still in the final stages of deregulation, but I understand that sunset comes very shortly, January 1, 1985. 2.5% of our total revenue comes from subsidized routes. We do not bid on any subsidies in any cities unless we feel that we can be self-sustaining within two years. Notwithstanding all the problems that deregulation spawned, I feel it did more for the overall service and competitive fares than what we had before. We can stimulate the market and be profitable without subsidies. By the way, subsidies are supposed to end in 1998.

Competition

Competition is not only something I enjoy, but also I believe it is necessary to produce a great product. I like the competitive environment. We have 18 non-competitive city segment routes that we operate in, out of about 50. In those 18, we keep our mind on the point that we could have competition at any time. Our major competitor in most of our cities in the Northwest is the automobile. Out of many of our cities, we get only about 30% of the people who travel on us to Portland or

Seattle. 70% drive their cars to either Portland or Seattle to pick up a flight to wherever.

Another major competitor we have in the Northwest is the other regional airline which covers a lot of our routes and would like to do more. The advantage that we have is that most regional airlines believe that their business is flying airplanes. That's just not the business at all. It is simply serving people. Those that do not have service as a priority may do okay, but it has to catch up with them some day.

We are rated about sixth of all the regional airlines in the country. Analysts too often rate us by the number of passengers we carry. Better they should rate us on profitability. Why don't they talk about earnings per share? Right now, we are marginal in this area. Everything is based on quantity, very rarely on quality. On quality, we are at the top. That's the thinking of most people who follow this industry. I've only been in it three years and I want to tell you it's some industry. In addition to the investment bankers, there are some analysts here, I understand, and you people who really analyze the industry ought to listen up to some of the things I'm talking about.

Keep in mind that the only thing left when you get off a plane is an empty ticket jacket and a memory of the service you received. Some of those memories are long-lived – good or bad. Our Company reinforces with our employee's excellent service to the public. We offer coffee and newspapers at the gate. Our competition across the way did the same two weeks later as a reaction. They copied us for the wrong reason. Airlines should get back to doing things for the right reasons. I'm told that 90% of the regional airlines were started by pilots and airplane nuts, or because someone or some group was looking for a tax shelter. In my view, those are not good reasons for starting an airline. By the way, there are 35 regional airlines in the west. When I look at that and see that we're one of the best financed, that's scary. But that's the competitive environment we are in.

In closing, let me pass on to you something I've heard before, which I believe to be right on the mark: "The way to make a small fortune in this business is to start out with a big one." Thank you.

Acquisition of Air Oregon

E veryone who can compute basic algebra knows that a minus times a minus is a plus. Whether or not that theory would work for Horizon, Kuolt and Sawyer were about to find out.

Their initial reaction to Bob Booth's query, "Do you want to buy an airline?" hadn't been encouraging for the chairman of Air Oregon. But Kuolt and Sawyer decided it wouldn't hurt to check out the operation.

"One thing to be said for Air Oregon," Bruce McCaw today recalls, "is that they had a very strong shareholder base that represented the Who's Who of the State of Oregon so the banks were just going along with them at the time. Bob Booth, a well-known broadcaster in Oregon, was on the board and an absolutely wonderful guy. There was a lot of mutual respect and we saw it as an opportunity to do something together rather than fighting each other for routes."

Horizon had put a lot of pressure on Air Oregon by flying competitively on some of their routes. Horizon's better airplanes and service later took its toll.

Horizon Air and Air Oregon
Now One Great Airline

On June 17th, 1982, Horizon Air and Air Oregon consolidated to become one airline—Horizon Air. To you, our passenger, this will mean better service, better schedules, and larger, more comfortable aircraft on certain segments in Oregon. With the consolidation of Horizon Air and Air Oregon, Horizon Air became the seventh largest regional carrier in the United States. We have built our reputation on providing exceptional in-flight beverage and snack service aboard our larger 40-passenger Fairchild F-27 Rolls Royce powered propjets. This service will now be available on certain Oregon routes.

We believe that the combination of the two airlines will provide you with substantially better service and better value.

We appreciate your patience and request your indulgence during this transitional period.

Thank you for flying Horizon Air.

"It is our privilege to serve you."

HORIZON AIR
"The Northwest's Regional Airline."

Call Your Travel Agent, Or Call Horizon Air.

Based on this cursory examination, McCaw and Kuolt flew down to Portland to meet both Booth and the carrier's president, Don Streun, who was more of a mild-mannered person with limited knowledge of the airline business. Streun, however, did have deep political connections. As they got to know one another, he and Kuolt became very compatible despite their opposite personalities. As with most of his close friends, Kuolt would call him by his last name.

This ability to get along was described by Dee Dee Maul as "a pair of CEOs who had tremendous respect from persons within their organizations. That resulted in a real partnership." This, she said later, helped the Air Oregon people to become 'Horizonized'.

Air Oregon had financed the airline through a local bank and the bank's chairman was on the board. This was a problem. Another reality was that all board members had signed personally for the airline. Collectively, they were on the hook for several million dollars. It was further apparent that no one had been minding the store as carefully as they should.

"It was such a 'club' deal that the outstanding debt had become so large it was going to wipe out some of these guys," McCaw observed. "There was no doubt it was a real dicey situation. Some had what could be called a major stake. Other influential shareholders had a lot to lose as well. Still, some could have lost several million dollars and survived."

Kuolt looked further at the airline and Sawyer perused the books.

"They are losing $300,000 plus a month, so between us, we are losing about $850,000 a month," Sawyer conveyed the bad news to Kuolt. "But, as I look at it, I believe that if we put the two airlines together, perhaps losses could be reduced for the combined operation. We're not in default yet with any of our agreements but all of Air Oregon's agreements are."

The team from Horizon said that the only way they could "do a deal" would be for the Oregon investors to provide the money for Horizon to buy them. This announcement was followed by stunned silence. The members of Air Oregon's board looked at one another in disbelief. After a few seconds, they were further informed that they would also have to provide the money to keep both operations alive. Again there was silence like The Night Before Christmas.

Andersen was the first to respond.

"Let's see if I have this straight. You don't have any money to buy us and you don't have any money to run the companies. So, why should we give you more money to do that?"

Sawyer was first to respond.

"Let's just say that if you don't lend us the money, you will continue to have your major losses at Air Oregon. So, at least this gives you one last shot."

There were no sound business reasons to loan, give or provide Horizon anything. But Air Oregon's investors had been meeting every month, poring over their operating losses and a negative cash flow of over $300,000. At those monthly meetings, they always agreed to write individual checks for about $25,000 to $30,000. They had been doing it for years and could see no end to it. It seemed, though, that their pride wouldn't let them pull the plug. To them, it was *the* Oregon Airline and they had their reputations to protect.

Sawyer tried to ease their pain, saying, "Look, if you lend us the money, you won't have to get together and write checks every month." *Great consolation.*

Air Oregon's board caucused. They assessed what they were losing and concluded, "How about we give you enough money to last about six months?"

Sawyer beamed, "Well, that's six months you won't have to get together as you are doing now."

"That's not a bad idea." Andersen answered for his board.

Now the ball was again in Horizon's court. Kuolt and Sawyer knew they now had to come up with a plan that would fly. Air Oregon's board was told that if they loaned the money, Milt would find other money and then "we can get the banks to go along with us."

Sawyer was now faced with writing a business plan from which no assumptions could be made that the combined operation would be in any way successful financially. The only thing number crunching would reveal was that, maybe, just maybe, losses for both carriers could be reduced about $150-$180 thousand a month, which at the time, was worth considering. What this amounted to was that the two together would only lose about $500,000 a month. But there was no way to forecast beyond that. Even extending his assumptions out a couple of years, there was no way Sawyer could shave the half a million figure.

Once a plan, as meager as it may have seemed, was set in motion, the banks went along. Again, Sawyer had to figure out how to get a good price for some of Kuolt's remaining assets. That in itself was not insurmountable but the time frame in which it had to be accomplished was challenging. Finally the Team Horizon did what they had set out to do. Now, on to Portland and the meeting with Air Oregon's board.

Sawyer characterized the board meeting as a "classic." He admits that the proposal Horizon was putting forth bordered on ridiculous. It was so inconclusive that even Kuolt wasn't sure he wanted to go to the meeting. But he went. All 12 of Air Oregon's board members were present.

Andy Andersen was first to speak. "We are going to consider a proposal from Horizon Air." He gave the floor to Sawyer. Sawyer had barely begun what would have been a long-winded explanation, when Andersen, a big Dane known throughout Oregon for his directness, interrupted.

"Excuse me, David. Let's get right to the bottom line here. What we have, gentlemen, is we have Horizon Air with a dose of the clap. And Air Oregon also has a dose of the clap. The question before us is do we accept the proposal in front of us and have a combined airline with twice as much clap, or, will we have the two claps cancel one another out. On that basis, I propose you vote *for* the proposal in front of you and we'll find out if we are going to have twice as much clap or no clap at all."

The vote was positive and the wheels were set in motion for the merging of the two airlines.

There were fewer losses to be sure, but they were still Horizon's losses. The deal closed. Kuolt got another $5 million based upon the decline in losses, plus some other financing and the combined operations were off and running. As aircraft fuel prices declined, Kuolt kept adding new cities to the route structure. This impacted the competition and some dropped by the wayside. Cascade Airways definitely felt the brunt of the combined Horizon Air-Air Oregon operation.

A huge reason for the successful merger was the synergy between Air Oregon's president, Don Streun and Milt Kuolt. The two had a good working relationship from day one. Although poles apart on personality, there was a wealth of mutual respect in the association. In a meeting, for instance, Kuolt would start grinding and Streun would sit listening, being very quiet and polished. Then Streun would put forth his viewpoint and Kuolt would say, "Okay, I'll buy that – I hadn't thought of it that way." Streun had a way of making a point with impeccable timing. He knew the right time to make a statement that would really stick with Milt. Or, Kuolt might respond, "Streun, I think you're really out to lunch on that. Here are my thoughts." And Streun would reply, "It will be tough, but maybe it will work." There was always that give and take.

Air Oregon's pilots trusted and respected Streun and were basically satisfied with their working conditions, even with the carrier's mounting losses. Prior to Horizon's acquisition, no fewer than 23 would-be carriers had preceded Air Oregon in the State of Oregon and all were defunct.

The integration of the two airlines happened gradually. In Medford, Air Oregon was running Horizon's ticket counter where employees started to get a feel for what the Seattle-based airline was all about. Dee Dee Maul, responsible for stations and agents, recalled that, "They really liked Horizon's style and that we displayed really great back walls and ticket counters and that our people looked good, had decent uniforms and great attitudes."

Blending two distinct working groups wasn't easy. Seniority within the merged group was addressed with an inventive one-for-two idea that gave consolation to Horizon's pilots while assuring Air Oregon's senior pilots that they wouldn't have to go to the end of the list. It was Tom Cufley's chore to introduce the blended list to Horizon's pilots who, for the most part, had been onboard with the first F-27s. There were some raised eyebrows with the Air Oregon contingent but the idea was accepted that if they were number five in seniority today, they could be higher tomorrow.

Alan "Z" Zanouzoski, who came aboard with Tom Cufley at Horizon's inception, recalls, "Air Oregon's Metroliner IIs and IIBs had inefficient anti-skid brakes, and required extra caution by pilots. After acquisition, our main task was to bring Air Oregon's pilots up to our proficiency standards. In the process, we learned that one of their pilots was not qualified to fly instruments. So, off he went immediately to ground school."

In those years, it was not uncommon for the airline to have as much as a fifty percent turnover with its pilots. Some would return to other carriers from which they had been furloughed, others would go on to Alaska Airlines. A story was that in Air Oregon's early years, some of their pilots actually paid the carrier for them to fly the Piper Navajos (forerunner to the Metroliner IIs) just to log flying time.

Essentially, it was Cufley and "Z" who kept the airline flying. The element of safety was paramount with them and one of the reasons they had such a good relationship with the FAA.

Bruce McCaw remembers that Air Oregon's Fairchild-Swearingen Metro II aircraft were a real nightmare to maintain. They had even more operational problems involving crew training. Air Oregon pilots had to recognize that their training had been lax, that time would have to be spent in simulators to get them up to speed on Horizon's procedures. Air Oregon pilots had been flying with an FAA Part 135 certified carrier which essentially meant an air taxi operation with smaller aircraft weighing under 12,500 pounds; anything from a Cessna 172 up to and including Metroliners. Now, with Horizon, they would have to meet FAA Part 121 standards. This also required that each Air Oregon pilot gain added proficiency in the Metroliners. Flying only one piece of equipment, Air Oregon pilots had to be upgraded into Horizon's system, bringing their training up to par with other similar carriers.

Air Oregon's co-pilots would spend some ten hours in the simulator for the initial checkout. This also allowed them to become proficient in emergency procedures without performing actual emergencies in training aircraft which created its own issues of safety.

There is always a sense of trepidation when one feels their company is going to be sold and, with the history of Air Oregon, their employees felt a certain amount of pride. All the Air Oregon stations and reservations personnel knew Don Streun on a first name basis. He was very close to his people. They were all close knit, including the pilots. There was an air of excitement with the Air Oregon people throughout the acquisition process.

With the blended operation it became immediately apparent that the combined fleet had to be scrutinized. Horizon's F-27s had to be upgraded to increase reliability and the Metroliner IIs that came with the Air Oregon acquisition would require engine upgrades and some modifications to make them more serviceable. Or, the alternative would be to replace the entire fleet.

McCaw started investigating the 19-seat market where the choices at that time were the Beech 1900, which he described as "a piece of junk." Cascade had the Beech 99s, 15-seat unpressurized aircraft which Beech was also trying to sell to Horizon. The British had the Jetstream, the old Handley Page that had been repowered by British Aerospace. Those were the choices.

"If the British had repowered the Jetstream and stretched it, it would have been okay," McCaw says, "but we just couldn't get their attention." And McCaw knew it would take years to get the attention of the British and even longer to get any action.

At the same time Beech was aligning themselves more and more with Cascade and Horizon really didn't want the 1900s.

McCaw got acquainted with the senior management of Swearingen in San Antonio. Jim Foody, who became close friends with McCaw, was the head of their sales and very willing to work with Horizon.

Before any deal could be made there had to be some give and take in thinking with Horizon's decision makers. Kuolt had some strong objections and Sawyer was worried about the financials. There were concessions made by each.

McCaw recalls the financing with Fairchild turned out to be very creative and was rolled into the five-year leasing package. Other manufacturers were finding themselves in deep trouble when they would, in effect, be lending money to their customers. The carriers would use it up and end up with over-financed airplanes.

An example was Cascade Airways which bought 748s under a federal loan guarantee program. "Those were the most expensive 748s ever built," McCaw reflects. "They were over-financed to the tune of 110-120 percent of their cost which put two million dollars into Cascade's till — and they couldn't make the payments. Then Beech came in and dealt with them for the BAC 1-11s and the Beech 1900s, making it a totally screwed up deal." Quite a contrast to Horizon's acquisitions of the F-27s which were priced right and based upon cash flow.

But the deal was made for Horizon to lease the Metroliner IIIs. And a good one it was. Horizon got the planes and some cash with a good spare parts inventory for each. Essentially, Horizon was getting the planes at wholesale but with a front-end load in the change of equipment.

"If you spend your money on that, you're using it wisely," McCaw said. "Cascade never did that. They used their money for day-to-day operations. We spent the money upgrading our pilots and acquiring spare parts to bring that airplane on line.

"We had a wonderful relationship with Fairchild and they really supported us. I think back fifteen years later that we didn't want more than a five-year lease at the time as we were concerned we'd be buying some other aircraft because there were so many new designs in the marketplace. But those designs were so slow in coming that it didn't happen the way we had anticipated."

Instead of five years, Horizon ended up flying the Metroliner IIIs for 15-16 years. And to top it off, Fairchild likely ended up selling over thirty airplanes and 15 years worth of spare parts; a great deal for the manufacturer.

Horizon didn't initially use flight simulators for its Metroliner pilots although it did for those who flew its F-27s. At the time, New York-based Flight Safety had the only Metro simulators located in Texas, where customers took delivery of aircraft, and they weren't being utilized to the maximum. The only way Horizon could access them was to pay a flat contract price of $5,000 per year for each pilot. Instead of that arrangement, Horizon wanted to rent the simulators with its instructors and its procedures. Flight Safety told McCaw of Horizon that they had never done that. So, McCaw countered with this proposal:

"We want to use your simulators but can't afford to do it the way you do it. We really need to do it with our own program and will guarantee 2,000 hours per year at $210 per hour."

Although Horizon was comfortable using the F-27 simulator back at US Air in Pittsburgh, it started doing the bulk of its training with Flight Safety. It was a very satisfying relationship.

It had been requested that de Havilland have a Dash 8 simulator at the outset. Horizon pushed to use Flight Safety which would later put simulators both in Seattle and Portland. It was a strong statement – reflecting the excellent working relationship with de Havilland.

McCaw says that it was a transition time – a critical time – for Horizon as it was evolving into a real professional airline and an investment had to be made in the future.

Time was taken to get the procedures right and the end result spoke for itself. Both entities went through some very trying times. And the Air Oregon folks really didn't want Horizon in their lives. They really wanted to keep doing the things their way and that simply didn't work. The rules had changed. Even with some disagreements, Horizon now owned the total operation and was going to run it *the Horizon way.*

With the Fairchild relationship, Horizon had the support of the manufacturer; and if something didn't work it was fixed. "We were running a 19-seat operation like we were doing the 40-seat operation." McCaw recalls. "Milt was all over my backside, but we were doing the right things."

After acquiring the new fleet, maintenance and training were the next considerations. Horizon really didn't have a satisfactory base in Seattle to maintain its F-27s. A deal to acquire the Western Airlines hangar never came to fruition. This made a Portland maintenance base even more important since there were two hangars to provide an immediate maintenance base more centrally located to Horizon's system.

Since, for the most part, the two airlines operated in separate cities with different hubs, there were no reductions in staff for the stations. From baggage handlers to maintenance, it was beginning to work.

One example was Kim Stockett who was about to quit Air Oregon when she saw the potential in the Horizon acquisition. A critical issue was the records section that involved parts inventories and other maintenance details. Kim quickly integrated the required essentials as did other employees who had accepted the status quo but now caught the vision that was Horizon Air.

A strong friendship exists today between Milt Kuolt and Andy Andersen as a result of the early days when Air Oregon was acquired. Andy was the only person of Air Oregon's original board who went on to Horizon's board of directors. Subsequently, Andy offered Milt advice that he sometimes took and other times did not, on occasion to Kuolt's regret.

Early on, one of the maintenance crew bailed from the Oregon base and took several others with him to America West. Dick Heaton, Horizon maintenance chief, said they were mainly people he could afford to lose.

The original investors in Air Oregon who took stock in Horizon and held it until the carrier was acquired by Alaska, essentially doubled their investment. But along the way it was somewhat like a high stakes poker game where you hold a hand you're not too sure about but are reluctant to drop out, hoping ultimately to share in the pot.

As Heaton began solidifying his maintenance team, he brought in Dave Treadway as chief inspector from Evergreen Airways. At the time, there were about 14 Metroliners and six F-27s to maintain. But still more F-27s were needed.

Again, Scott Kidwell did his globetrotting to find more aircraft. The next one was found in Saskatoon,

Saskatchewan; another had been in the Hughes Airwest operation. The next F-27 was found in Miami. It had been brought up from Nicaragua, complete with bullet holes. Yet another was out of Africa.

On January 27, 1983, the Oregon Economic Development Commission approved $3.1 million in industrial development bonds for purchasing and refurbishing the most recently found F-27s. With that announcement, the Portland Oregonian reported that the capital provided "could result in as many as 15 new jobs in the Portland area where the company has its reservations and maintenance operations." Also, as reported in the article, "Horizon serves the Oregon cities of Portland, Eugene/Springfield, Salem, Medford, North Bend/Coos Bay, Redmond/Bend and Klamath Falls. It also serves Seattle, Yakima, Pasco and has three weekly round trips to Sun Valley." During the early petitioning for revenue bonds, Horizon had dangled the carrot that it was also considering moving its corporate headquarters to Portland.

Although corporate headquarters remained in Seattle, flight operations were centered in Portland, which also became a primary hub, accommodating the reservations center and maintenance and a base for flight crews.

Meet to Fix

Standardizing the Horizon fleet was just one problem. Placing the right people in the correct slots was another. This called for a top-level strategy session, one away from the daily distractions of the home office. Hawaii was the destination as company executives went into their closed-door meeting.

It was apparent that the company had to be reorganized. Unanticipated rapid growth with the acquisition of Air Oregon had caused rampant frustration. To top it all off, Kuolt was on the warpath. Boxes were being filled in on the organization chart with an element of uncertainty.

"We had outgrown ourselves and everybody was frustrated," McCaw recalls. "The Air Oregon acquisition was just behind us. Prominent among the boxes that needed filling was VP of operations. I said the best person, if we can get him, is Chuck Hall, formerly director of operations for Standard Airways in Seattle and currently was with Japan Airlines. Both Dick Heaton and Joe Clark knew him well."

By the end of the meeting, it was determined that all the boxes had to be filled. Today. McCaw tried to call Hall from the Honolulu hotel and learned he was on a trip to Tokyo. Dave Sawyer then got up and wrote "McCaw" in the box for VP of operations. All present agreed with the appointment.

McCaw immediately started to work on very serious problems with maintenance. Primarily, the FAA was on Horizon's back as systems reliability was beginning to fall apart. McCaw went to Hal Morrell, Regional Head of the FAA and laid his cards on the table. "You've got to give me time to fix it. Milt Kuolt needs to be convinced how important all these internal problems are. We have a mix of aircraft and had to defer certain maintenance items. Essentially, I need time to deal with these things and I ask that you not shut us down.

"Gus Robinson was president of Alaska at the time and they were helping us with spares. Next, we got the pilots to think more cohesively as a team. This group had been writing up stuff that wasn't broken. Those were the real critical things."

By late 1982, McCaw's job was to get Milt Kuolt out of operations and allow the people there to get their act together.

It was but a week after the Air Oregon acquisition that a big management meeting was held in Sun Valley. McCaw had to make the presentation for operations that included dispatch and records. He didn't know a lot of the Air Oregon people since Horizon's maintenance had been merged into theirs. The greatest disparity was that Air Oregon was an FAA Part 135 operation and Horizon was a Part 121. Horizon had the F-27s and Air Oregon had the Metroliners. Air Oregon's chief pilot didn't want to listen to Tom Cufley, Horizon's chief pilot; and Milt Kuolt was calling them "hardasses." To top it all off, the blended operation was flying under the most challenging conditions: old aircraft.

McCaw stayed as VP -operations until George Bagley came in with the Transwestern of Utah acquisition. George, in time, took over the responsibility, although McCaw was still handling parts of it up until the airline was sold to Alaska.

During this period, McCaw had a number of titles, including planning, operations and strategy. Major challenges included gaining commonality of parts and standardizing the fire warning systems for the F-27s to enhance their reliability. He also got to know the guys at Fairchild quite well. Ed Swearingen had designed the Metroliner. With his contacts in San Antonio, McCaw went to Fairchild to look at the 10-UA engines that would enhance the Metroliner's performance. The upgrades would be a distinct advantage at some of the airports when higher temperature would prevent scheduling the older aircraft with adequate passenger loads. *But what was really needed were new airplanes.*

Through all of this, Kuolt would frequently listen to McCaw's advice which ultimately resulted in an even greater relationship between the two men. McCaw would do things Kuolt was directly opposed to and Kuolt would slam his hands on the table and yell, "We are not going to do that!" But, through it all, Kuolt didn't overreact even as McCaw would go around him, realizing it was sometimes easier to just go ahead and do it.

Finding Aircraft and Parts

S cott Kidwell put together another deal for five F-27s in Bolivia. One had crashed into the mountains with a soccer team aboard. It was 72 days before they would be rescued but the plane was still on the airline's status board with an "X" through it. Horizon was going to buy the remaining four aircraft for $450,000 each. There was only one problem. Everyone in the South American company had to get a cut of the deal. It was doubtful that the airline would realize even $50,000 after the transaction when one director, then another would want their cut. About the time Horizon's team was ready to get a plane out of the country, someone else would want a cut, screwing up the whole deal.

Fokker F-28

The first pure jet in the Horizon fleet was a Fokker F-28 that came from the Gold Coast of Africa. It arrived in July 1984. A

Plane maintenance. (Courtesy Ron Suttell)

problem was integrating it into the system, especially with the former Air Oregon pilots who had previously flown only Metroliners. Flight simulator time was a requirement for anyone upgrading to the pure jet. The plane was placed into service before the end of the month flying between Seattle, Pasco, Boise and Portland.

Now the parts inventory necessary to maintain several types of aircraft became quite significant. An outside consulting firm was invited in to perform an inventory analysis. They created quite a flap by telling Milt Kuolt that someone in Horizon's maintenance crew had made a monumental mistake buying unserviceable parts. Kuolt went into orbit. It wasn't all that serious. Truth of the matter was that many of the parts had come out of Canada and were tagged with the same green color as the American repairable parts. But as soon as the tags were changed to their appropriate colors, the problem was resolved.

Heaton announced to David Sawyer that with all the F-27s added to the fleet, he had to buy some more parts and he had a deal for some in Cucamonga, Bolivia.

"So what do you want to do?" Sawyer asked Heaton.

"Look, this is one hell of a deal. I want to go down there and buy these parts," Heaton implored.

"So, how much money are we talking about?"

"About a quarter-million dollars." Although the money crunch had ameliorated a bit, it was still a lot of money at the time.

"Only a quarter-million. Is that all?" Sawyer asked.

"Yes, I'm thinking of going to Bolivia at the end of the week and I'll need to take the money with me."

"Then you are going to need a check?"

"No, I need cash."

"Let me see if I have this straight. You need a quarter-million in cash to go to Cucomonga, Bolivia?"

"Yeah."

"Well, why don't you wait here a minute." Sawyer rushed over to Kuolt's office where he addressed the Chief.

"Milt, your buddy, Dick Heaton in the maintenance department wants to go to Cucomonga, Bolivia to get some parts for the F-27s."

"Well, we probably need them, don't we?"

"Yeah, but Heaton wants me to give him a quarter-million dollars. In cash."

Milt's head whipped around. "In cash! What the hell is he talking about? Why does he need cash?" Sawyer had already prepared a check request because he wasn't comfortable giving Heaton or anyone that much cash.

"You're chief financial officer. It's your decision," Kuolt hit the ball back into Sawyer's court. Kuolt wouldn't sign the check request, which left Sawyer holding the bag. So Sawyer went to Seafirst bank to get the quarter-million in cash.

"It seems we had about $250,004 in the account. It took every dime we had," Sawyer recalls.

"How long will you be gone?" Sawyer nervously asked Heaton.

"I won't be gone long. I should be back in about four days."

Heaton departed the office on a Friday. Monday rolled around and Sawyer barely gave it a thought. Then came

Tuesday and Wednesday. Sawyer's anxiety began to build and he started making calls. "Has anyone heard from Dick?" No one had. "Does anyone know where he is staying?" No one knew. Thursday and Friday rolled around. No Heaton.

"Kuolt inquired of Sawyer, "Where in the hell is Dick and how did he do?

"He hasn't come back."

"Then where the hell is my money?" Milt demanded.

"Your money is with Dick, wherever Dick is," knowing very well that wouldn't ease Kuolt's anxiety. Thirteen and fourteen days went by. Now more than a few at the home office were getting antsy. Imaginations went wild; some thinking Heaton was the only smart one here. After all, he had $250,000 in cash and was headed for Bolivia. About then, Sawyer was beginning to think Bolivia might be a good place for him to go as well since the bank account had been drained.

On the fourteenth day, Sawyer's phone rang. It was Heaton. "Dave, I just got back last night and I want to come over and see you." Sawyer had made it company policy that everyone turn in their expenses within three days following travel.

When Heaton arrived, Sawyer asked, with some trepidation, "Well, how was the trip, Dick?"

"Fine. Just fine," was the response as Heaton handed Sawyer his expense slips. "Listen, I know you always want these itemized but these weren't."

Glancing at the receipts, Sawyer exclaimed, "You're gone for fourteen days and you spent only $200? Dick, what did you eat?"

"Oh, I ate well. Steaks. Drinks. Everything."

"Well, that's just great." And Heaton got up to leave.

"Dick. You forgot something."

"What's that?"

"The $250,000."

"Oh, the airplane parts."

"Yeah, the airplane parts."

Heaton muttered "Yes," tossing Sawyer a piece of paper on which had been scribbled, "Miscellaneous airplane parts, $250,000."

"It came out exactly even?" Sawyer stared blankly.

"Yeah."

"Gee, Dick. Can you help me out a bit? What do we have? What sort of parts?"

"Oh, a lot of parts," Heaton reassured Sawyer whose blood pressure was rising.

"Okay. Do I write 'a lot of parts' down? Or can we be more specific? Do we have propellers, for example?"

"Oh, yeah. We have propellers."

"How many propellers?"

"I don't know."

"Wheels?"

"Yeah, we got wheels."

The long and the short of it was that the entire Cucomonga purchase went into the company's books as "miscellaneous airplane parts, $250,000." That accounting entry came into question following the acquisition by Alaska some years later. It was, in the end, accepted that Horizon Air got a lot of parts and it came out exactly at $250,000.

After that incident, Sawyer often thought that if things didn't go so well in the future, he could always go to Cucomonga, Bolivia and live for $10 a day.

GIs learned in World War II that the first ones into a new country were able to bargain quite well with the natives but those who arrived later would be up against an experienced, much more savvy populace. The same was true for Heaton on a subsequent trip to Bolivia. By that time, Boeing was doing its high altitude test work on its 757 in LaPaz. A meal had previously cost the lira equivalent of about 30 cents and the Boeing men were leaving $5 tips. The food establishments and hotels quickly picked up on this and a hotel room that had been about

40 lira per day was bumped up to 700 lira. Heaton was left uncomfortably short of cash. Credit cards were unacceptable and trying to pass a check was a joke. Bank transfers wouldn't work because they took ten to twelve days to process.

One night, the guy dining next to Heaton was a Boeing supervisor. In conversation, Heaton remarked that he could sure use an extra $600-$700 as he was in real trouble. The Boeing guy loaned Heaton some traveler's checks to tide him over with a gentlemen's agreement he would be repaid when Heaton got back to the States.

Bolivia is known for its potent tea. In fact, some people say they get a buzz from drinking it. Heaton thought that for a buck and half a pack, he could get about 15-20 packs to take home. The tea proved to be so potent that the aroma from the packets spread through the airplane. It dawned on Heaton that when they landed in Miami, Customs would likely throw him in the slammer. Before touching down, he flushed the tea down the lavatory. Knowing what had happened to Heaton's tea, when Heaton came to the Boeing guy's home to repay the loan, he handed Heaton some Bolivian tea and then poured him a cup.

In four trips to Bolivia, Kidwell and Heaton only managed to get out with one airplane. Something always seemed to foul up the deal.

Horizonation

Other elements to be combined with the Air Oregon acquisition involved reservations. Air Oregon had a system more sophisticated than Horizon's. It was the Braniff "Cowboy" reservations system, tailored to the needs of commuter airlines at that time. Although the switch over of phones and computers presented an enormous challenge, it was completed satisfactorily. The changeover involved literally flipping a switch and transferring Horizon's system to Portland on one Saturday night.

Dee Dee Maul believes another factor in the successful merger was that Air Oregon personnel were so quick to become acclimated to Horizon's style and corporate culture. She performed all new hire orientation programs. And when Milt couldn't come in and address groups himself, Dee Dee had a videotape in which he welcomed the new hires and conveyed his corporate philosophy and personal commitment to service. It was the beginning of "Horizonation." Maul recalled, "It was kind of like homogenized milk. We were going to Horizonize you. It really clicked. It made people feel they were as welcome as a good friend."

After nearly 17 years, there are many former Air Oregon people still working for Horizon, including pilots and station personnel. One rose to chief pilot and another to senior vice president of operations.

Now, with things humming along a bit better, Horizon went looking to see what else was out there to be acquired. The spotlight focused on Transwestern Airlines of Utah.

Acquisition of Transwestern

Transwestern was a reprise of the earlier scenario with Air Oregon. It was losing money and for sure, Horizon still wasn't making any. Again the premise, if the two were put together, they would lose less.

Making it work required going back to the same banks and the same people and presenting to them a new plan. But the truth of the matter was there had never been a forecast that would show the airlines would be successful even though they cut operating losses. One thing was apparent, that by adding Transwestern, they would have as many different types of aircraft as a South American revolution.

The principal players at Transwestern were president George Bagley, a former Air Force pilot and the carrier's chairman, Larue Harcourt, a sports promoter. Harcourt wore many hats. He was a business agent for professional athletes; he negotiated contracts; was involved in many limited partnerships and leased aircraft to Transwestern. Bagley had followed the

George Bagley

acquisition of Air Oregon and learned that in the blending Horizon and Air Oregon operations, there were some Metro II commuter aircraft for sale. Bagley contacted Scott Kidwell who was primarily responsible for acquiring aircraft. And Bagley ended up talking with Milt Kuolt.

Bagley called the Chief and said, "I understand you like to buy airlines." Transwestern, at the time, had about a dozen aircraft consisting of a mixture of Metro IIs and Beech C-99s plus one Twin Otter. It's route structure served Salt Lake and Logan, Grand Junction, Sun Valley, Pocatello, Boise and Idaho Falls. The Sun Valley connection was a viable market for Transwestern and it was a factor that attracted Kuolt to the operation.

Bagley admits that, at the time, he didn't really understand Horizon's acquisition of Air Oregon. But that was secondary. His immediate concern was finding a home for Transwestern which was too small and undercapitalized to survive over the long haul. Initially, he didn't see any role for himself in the acquisition. However, during the transition, Bagley spent an increasing amount of time in Seattle, learning more about Kuolt and his carrier's operation. When the position of VP of flight operations came open, it was Bagley who filled the slot. Char Green, whom Bagley would later marry, also came to Horizon with the Transwestern acquisition. She became an integral part of the carrier's sales team.

It didn't take long for Bagley to discover that Horizon was a vibrant, energetic operation made up of dedicated individuals absolutely intent on making the carrier a success. Following deregulation, the early 1980's were a period in which everyone was relearning the game.

"Early on, I think everyone was trying to figure out what deregulation meant for the entire industry," Bagley reflected. "My thinking at the time was that it was going to evolve into about four or five airlines. There would be a red one, blue one, green one, a white one or something like that. And, I thought these industry survivors would have hotels, rental cars and would manage a passenger's entire travel experience.

"I was wrong. That never came to pass. Who could foresee the role the regional carrier would play? We were all learning."

Indeed. United Airlines' attempt at total services integration under its Allegis banner failed. In the process, it severely impacted the carrier and its Western International Hotels subsidiary.

"For the most part, Transwestern people who made the transition blended in well with Horizon's operation. More than sixteen years later, former Transwestern employees can be found in Horizon at its stations, in accounting, dispatch and on the flight deck," says Bagley who in 1995 was named president and CEO of Horizon Air.

Growing Pains

S un Valley. A magic name. It was a location that always captivated Milt Kuolt. Why not? Ever since Averell Harriman ran his railroad there in the 1930s, it has been the choice destination of the rich and famous. Its scenery is spectacular. Its stream fishing, some of the finest in the world. And skiers were flocking to Sun Valley long before many of the other popular ski resorts sprung up in the west. Although it was Milt Kuolt's decision to go into Sun Valley, it was Joe Clark's idea, which is one of the reasons he was called "Sun Valley Joe." Joe, an avid skier, believed that Sun Valley as a "resort destination" would make Horizon look more credible than competitor Cascade Airways which served only the eastern Washington points.

Those who chose to fly into Hailey, Idaho, the closest airport to Sun Valley, did so when they could find a window in the weather. Often pilots were admonished to "watch the turbulence going in!" Essentially, that is what Andy Andersen warned Milt Kuolt about when Horizon's president indicated a personal desire to buy the Elkhorn Resort in Sun Valley.

Dee Dee Maul remembers going to Elkhorn with Kathy, Milt and Bruce McCaw when the resort was closed "like a ghost town." The real estate agent opened up the front doors to the resort's lobby. It was dark and cold.

Kathy, sharing the excitement of Sun Valley, looked at Dee Dee and said, "I am going to put the most beautiful Christmas tree in this lobby."

When Milt decided to go into the Valley, it was partly due to Kathy's excitement about the area. She loved it there and it wasn't because of what Sun Valley represents to some as the "playground of the rich and famous." She

loved the beauty of the area, the majesty of virgin snow and the blue-sky days.

Andy Andersen has been a savvy businessman for over half a century. He knows where to make money, especially in pioneering tilt-up concrete construction techniques. He also has a good sense for where money can be lost and he was not at all bashful of reminding Kuolt of that fact. But Elkhorn was something Kuolt had to experience for himself. He believed that if the Valley had a significant upgrade in air service, passenger traffic would soar. An attractive resort destination would make it even better. He said he was the one to make that happen and set about beginning the task.

The first two winters he owned the resort, little if any snow came to the Valley. Skiers went to Aspen and elsewhere. Kuolt poured millions more into the resort over and above his initial purchase price. There was no doubt it was a first class facility with one of the most highly rated golf courses in the west. Its Robert Trent Jones golf course rates among the nation's top 50. Andy Andersen, who opposed Milt buying the Elkhorn Lodge, introduced him to Jeff Steury who became the Director of Golf and ran one of the finest golf programs in Idaho. Problems relating to transportation into the Valley had sunk previous owners of Elkhorn but Kuolt, undaunted, was prepared to give it his best shot.

When the winter snows returned, there was not enough occupancy to make the resort consistently profitable. Fifteen years and many millions later, Kuolt bailed. Despite his heavy loss in Elkhorn, it was a unique experience, albeit a costly one. *Even the great players sometimes have to leave their chips on the table and walk away.*

One of the many legacies Milt Kuolt left the Valley was much improved and more frequent air service. Sun Valley was one of the earliest cities added to Horizon's destinations out of Seattle.

Intrepid Tom Cufley remembers the inaugural flight into Sun Valley. Friedman Memorial Airport at Hailey was governed by Instrument Flight Regulations. But without an instrument landing system, a pilot aid essential to flying in bad weather, it presented a real challenge. The weather was horrible. Visibility was down to one mile and blowing snow. He and co-pilot Alan Zanouzoski were at the controls, concentrating intently on coping with the turbulence, their minds racing ahead to the landing. Skis were packed into every available niche in the F-27. The passengers were having a grand time, oblivious to mounting concern in the cockpit. Coming up to the Magic

Reservoir intersection designated on the charts, the crew saw that the weather was still really bad in Sun Valley. Descending to the lowest altitude possible, Cufley finally had visual contact with the surface.

"Alan, why don't you cancel our IFR flight clearance with the FAA and we'll take a visual approach," Cufley suggested calmly but firmly to his co-pilot. John Cox, a Horizon employee, was sitting in the cockpit jump seat and from his vantage point, the weather looked even worse. By now, the heavily loaded aircraft was down to about 400 feet above the surface when Cufley spotted a familiar road that he knew was by a hill that led directly into the Valley.

"Alan, just tell me when you see the hill," Cufley barked.

"What hill?" A confused Cox implored from the jump seat.

Alan was first with visual contact. "There it is! We're coming up on it now!"

Relieved, Cufley turned the corner and set up for final approach into Hailey. Usually personnel from another carrier into the area provided ground support for Horizon but on this bad weather day, the airport was essentially closed.

Touch down was smooth as silk. All passengers blissfully deplaned. *Just another uneventful trip into Sun Valley.*

Horizon clientele into Sun Valley were not the usual business commuters going back and forth between Seattle and Pasco and Seattle and Yakima. These flyers brought steamer trunks and four or five fur coats for the week in the Valley. The adage, "The passenger is always right" was tested to its limits when, as often happened, all the baggage accompanying the passenger wouldn't fit on the same airplane in which they were traveling.

"You don't tell someone going to Sun Valley for a week or ten days vacation that they are allowed only two checked bags and one carry-on." said Dee Dee Maul. "I mean, besides their skis, they had ski clothes, boots, trunkloads of fur coats; traveling very, very bulky!"

Extra baggage was flown into Salt Lake, then bused to Sun Valley. Any baggage that could not be accommodated in that way just had to wait for the next flight, that is, if it had extra cargo space. Even Horizon with its reputation for great service couldn't help that. Some passengers understood. Some didn't.

Horizon general counsel, Art Thomas, who joined the airline about two years after its inception, remembers when Kuolt had scheduled a high level planning meeting in the middle of winter at Sun Valley. When the flight, carrying Thomas and other department heads reached Boise, they were informed that they would be flying no further because Hailey was below airline minimum weather conditions. Well, when a little thing like weather threatens to keep you from flying to a meeting scheduled by Milt Kuolt, you get there by some other means. So the team rented a station wagon. Ever eager Horizon ticket counter personnel seized the opportunity when they learned Thomas had rented a vehicle. They immediately loaded it with all the sidelined baggage it would carry.

The party arrived late at Elkhorn for the meeting. Without asking what kept them, Kuolt began grinding on Thomas for being late. But that was Kuolt.

From the beginning of service to Sun Valley, it was obvious Hailey Airport needed to update its approach aids. An Instrument Landing System was both too expensive and impractical due to terrain limitations. But a newly developed Microwave Landing System was thought to be the answer. While work began on the MLS before Alaska acquired Horizon, the one million-dollar system did not become operational until 1987. It resulted in lowered minimums for takeoffs and landings and facilitated better nighttime operations, but not by much. Neither the FAA nor the system's manufacturer ever attained the weather minimums expected from the installation.

Enter the Unions

M ilt Kuolt's philosophy is, "If you treat people right, they won't need to organize." Good theory. But even when employees are compensated fairly and commensurate with their industry, it is inevitable that certain groups believe they will fare better with collective bargaining.

The first union representation was with the Air Oregon acquisition and its mechanics at the Portland base, where the union was already in place.

"Actually, the maintenance union at Air Oregon really became an asset," Co-founder and Director Bruce McCaw said later. "This was an area where Horizon was most vulnerable because traditionally this industry segment is always highly organized."

Despite having a contract with Horizon, membership

in the mechanic's union over time experienced a steady decline. McCaw and others worked to limit Kuolt's direct contact with the union because his vehement opposition to organizing just fueled the fire. On one occasion, Milt got into it big time in the office with Transport Workers. Both McCaw and Sawyer worried that chaos would result. This confrontation was ultimately settled by cooler heads; and an amicable agreement was reached. Still, the mechanics, led by shop steward Gene Swan, were not totally satisfied.

While not a union matter, some employees' attitudes just didn't fit with Horizon's or, most specifically, Milt Kuolt's philosophy. One day, Dick Heaton called Kuolt and said he had a mechanic who wanted to talk with him and could he bring the guy up to Seattle as he had some specific questions.

"What does he want to talk about?" Kuolt asked.

"I don't know what this guy is going to say," Heaton responded, "but I have an idea what he is going to ask you."

Heaton brought the mechanic to Seattle and ushered him into Kuolt's office. The guy began his spiel.

"You know, Milt, I have only been working here a couple weeks and here it is December and we've had some snow and I was just wondering about the snow policy in this company."

Heaton turned away, knowing what was coming.

"Snow policy?" Kuolt interjected.

"Yes, you see the airline where I was most recently employed had a snow policy and I wonder if you could tell me what Horizon's is?"

"Horizon's *what*?"

"Snow policy. Where I last worked, the policy was that if I got to work at 8:00 and it started snowing at 9:00 – and it was still snowing an hour later at 10:00, we were allowed to leave and still get paid for a half-day. And if, for instance, it started snowing at 12:00 and quit during the day we would stay for the rest of the day. But, if it started snowing at 1:00 and there was an inch on the ground at 3:00, then we were allowed to go home and were paid for the rest of the day. So, do you have a snow policy around here?"

This was no *snow job*. The mechanic was serious.

"Yeah, I really do," Kuolt retorted. "I don't give a damn how much snow is out there. If you work, you get paid. If you want to go home, you don't get paid. That's my snow policy."

End of conversation. Heaton quickly ushered the guy out and caught the next flight back to Portland. While it likely wasn't the answer the mechanic was seeking, undoubtedly he got the message that *things were different here.*

To resolve other differences, McCaw headed to San Francisco for a meeting with the Transport Workers. It was hoped that a contract renewal could be successfully negotiated and both sides agreed to meet alternately in Seattle and San Francisco.

On the way from San Francisco International Airport to the union location, a little magic happened. McCaw took a cab and, unfamiliar with the area, tried to explain to the driver where the address was; that it was near Millbrae, a small industrial center near the freeway. As they continued, the driver was still uncertain of the address and McCaw was concerned that they would make it on time. Finally, the driver asked McCaw if, by any chance, he was going to meet with a union.

"Yeah, with the Transport Workers," McCaw responded.

"Hey! That's my union!" The driver was surprised.

"They have the cabbies organized down here?"

"No, I am a Pan Am mechanic and I've been driving cab for five years since I was laid off from Pan Am."

"Interesting."

McCaw walked into the meeting place and was asked if he had any trouble finding it. "No, he replied, "One of your members drove me over."

"But we don't represent cab drivers," was the response.

"No, he's a Pan Am mechanic and he's laid off." Then, in a surprisingly assertive tone, he added. "You know, we don't really want to put a bunch of your guys out there driving cabs. Instead, we'd like to get them back to work."

With that, McCaw presented the company's offer, saying, "It's the best we can do. Take it or leave it." The agreement was signed in ten minutes and McCaw was on his way back to Seattle.

Even with an agreement, mechanics union membership continued to drop so low that Horizon actually had to urge some to bring their dues current. The airline was concerned that if the contract was canceled for lack of union participation, it could be replaced by one much worse.

Although Air Oregon pilots didn't have formal union representation, they did have their own in-house association. Kuolt called a meeting with that group's attorney.

They met in Horizon's old offices on 188th Street, south of SeaTac. The air was definitely *hot*. Air Oregon's pilots loved their company and the Horizon acquisition was fraught with uncertainties. However, even though at one point in the discussion, Kuolt told the pilot's counsel he would throw him through his office window, negotiations settled down and differences were resolved.

Day By Day With Knolt

Milt had pet names for various employee entities, some of them uncomplimentary. Once he almost caused a riot when he suggested at a meeting of Portland flight attendants that trained monkeys could perform their tasks. His audience was livid.

It was a shoot from the lip response because he was irritated that the group was talking unions. He hadn't intended for his remark to come across in the manner in which it was received. What he really meant was that monkeys could be trained technically to do their job – pouring and serving drinks. But, that it took real people to provide the added personal caring element, "it is a privilege to serve you." A monkey couldn't do that.

But he didn't say that. He stormed out of the meeting as his anger level was beginning to escalate. He had sensed through body language and emotions that a riot might be in the offing.

Dee Dee Maul, out of the room when that reference was made, said, "Did we ever pay for that! It took weeks to clean up the mess."

The realization was setting in with the flight attendants that it just wasn't the same company any more. As will happen with many companies on a fast growth track, where everyone had been "family" and close, Horizon was getting to the size where it wasn't like that any more.

When the airline was in its embryonic stage, Milt could have everyone to his house and there was real camaraderie. The cord had been broken and many didn't want to lose that feeling.

"So," Maul observes, "Milt's statement sort of pushed them over the edge and they started to look at their CEO differently. And he would probably agree that he had reached the point where he couldn't keep his arms around the entire operation."

Somebody thought up the idea that perhaps a "mood meter" might be mounted outside the door to Kuolt's office with an arrow indicating different zones. Green, yellow and red might represent the different times of the day. Milt was often in the office at 4:30 a.m. This was constructive time for the early riser. By noon, it was definitely "approach with caution." Around three o'clock, "forget it." Then, about 4 p.m. out would come the rum and coke. When things were totally relaxed, again more constructive time would follow, strategizing with senior staff.

Dee Dee recalls Milt's siestas. "He would take this 15 to 20 minute nap. Sometimes he would wake up grouchy. Then about fifteen minutes later, he'd be fine. The nap was what kept him going. His days began very early. And, it was usually Joanne Traska, Milt's administrative assistant, who would awaken him. When Traska couldn't be there she would delegate someone else. I didn't want to be the one to awaken him prematurely, but it seemed I always got stuck with the task."

Bruce McCaw says it was Kuolt who built synergism into the team. "Many companies still don't get it. There is no synergy between senior and front line people. They fail to receive the message. Often the rank and file have to be re-apprised of the corporation's goals and reminded of the company's mission statement. When people fail to support the mission statement or to grasp their individual role in the execution of the plan, chaos results. To build a cohesive working force, the direction has to come from the top." Milt would say to his senior people, "Your actions are so loud, I can't hear a thing you're saying."

During this difficult time and to try to lighten things up, Tom Cufley thought it was time for Milt to get better acquainted with exactly what it took to fly an airplane. Kuolt had just been all over Cufley about the pilot group, complaining of this and that.

"Okay, Milt. I have to take this F-27 from SeaTac over to Boeing Field and you can fly the right seat." Cufley had tried once before, unsuccessfully, to get Milt to fly up front, so he was pleased when he accepted the invitation.

Airborne, Cufley took his hands off the controls and smiled at Kuolt. "There now. You just keep flying. We'll go by your house and then you can make a turn toward final for Boeing's north-south runway. Got it?"

Kuolt's demeanor belied any anxiety he may have felt inside as Cufley assisted along the way and during landing. After that flight, there was a lot less commentary from Kuolt about "prima donna" pilots. Kuolt enjoyed a good rapport with the pilots. They respected him. It was out of respect for their CEO that those matters which would have constituted upsetting union issues for other carriers, were settled in-house at Horizon. Many of the pilots "hung in" with Horizon, even during the tough times when they could have bolted to other airlines. An example is Jim Roberts, who joined Horizon in 1982 and is still flying today, now a captain on one of the carrier's F-28s.

Horizon's employees understood that the airline earnestly tried to give them every benefit they could. In the process, however, the Company had to survive. It did – while others were going under.

Father and son team flying for Horizon in 2000. Jim Roberts, left, began flying with Horizon in the early years. Jim and his son Adam are both captains on Horizon's F-28 jets.

Competitor Cascade

Everyone told Milt Kuolt that the airline business was a market share business. Milt did not like sharing the market. He wanted *all* the market. After digesting the Air Oregon and Transwestern acquisitions, Horizon was dominant in the Pacific Northwest commuter market. Its only competition was Cascade Airways, which was struggling, although Kuolt knew that if certain conditions could be met, it might make sense to acquire it. Kuolt says he knew from day one that Horizon had Cascade beat, that from a business vantage point, Cascade was bent on self-destructing. He had a quotation from on his office wall that said:

And they copied and copied and copied, but they couldn't copy my mind, so I left them sweating and stealing a year and half behind.

Bruce Kennedy, retired CEO of Alaska Airlines, remembers seeing the quotation at his first visit to Milt's office and his favorable impression.

With visitors, Milt would nod to the quotation and say, "See, that's the gumshoes with the competition."

Horizon literally rolled out the red carpet down the gate concourse when going into a city such as Yakima or Pasco. Next, out came the beautiful stainless steel coffee urns filled with the best of blends, along with real cream and sugar. Complimentary Wall Street Journals could be picked up with free coffee. Cascade made lame attempts to copy Horizon, prompting Dee Dee Maul to comment later, "I don't think they even knew *why* they were doing these things. They didn't have that spirit of intention or commitment to do it for the right reasons, so it never came off being good for them."

The same was true for equipment. Horizon was now flying a very nice airplane, pressurized for on-time operations back and forth over the Cascade Mountains. When Cascade realized Horizon was for real, they went out and bought two brand new Hawker 748s at about $6-8 million each. Even full passenger loads would have been insufficient to service their debt. To further illustrate Cascade's desperate measures to catch up, they next acquired five BAC1-11s, one of which was stripped for parts to keep the others flying. Because of Cascade's widely known heavy debt load, some in the industry referred to their new planes as "BAC1-*Chapter* 11s."

Milt Kuolt's friends love him. His enemies are few and often have little to say except that they are bewildered by some of his actions. Some call him arrogant and abrasive. Mark Chestnutt, former CEO of Cascade Airways said he has some objective and subjective opinions of Milt Kuolt, none of which he would state, other than to acknowledge Kuolt as "ruthless in his zeal to dominate the market and to succeed."

Bruce McCaw remembers first meeting Mark Chestnutt in 1968 when Chestnutt's father financed the first airplane for what then was Air Pacific. "George Chestnutt essentially bought the airplane, a Beech 99, so his son, Mark, could fly it, guaranteeing Mark a job with Air Pacific. The fledgling carrier only lasted about thirty days before re-emerging as West Pacific which struggled on for a year or more before failing.

"I believe Mark thought he was entitled to have the entire Pacific Northwest to himself and resented Horizon's presence. He cared deeply about Cascade but never quite understood what it took to be successful."

Despite what people said about Milt Kuolt, according to McCaw, "Mark Chestnutt was a difficult person. Kuolt was determined to be successful and never out specifically to kill Cascade. Chestnutt was always *reacting* to Horizon. When Horizon unwisely wet-leased (with pilots, etc. included) a DC-9, Chestnutt went out and made the fateful decision to acquire the BAC1-11s."

McCaw says that Cascade never seemed to operate with the thought that the money they borrowed had to be paid back; flying on a day-to-day basis, running out of a cash register. Everything Horizon did was calculated on it making economic sense. Another upstart competitor, also flying BAC 1-11s, Pacific Express was running $10 fares from Medford to San Francisco.

In analyzing a potential new market, John Cox of Horizon would carefully study traffic figures – fares were then based on returns needed to be profitable but low enough to stimulate traffic.

Being first on the scene, the competition could have done everything that Horizon would ultimately do. Evidence of this was that Horizon was able to get such key people from Cascade as Dee Dee Maul and Tom Cufley.

"In retrospect, we did try hard to put the acquisition

of Cascade together. Milt was determined and we worked hard in the negotiations. The combination could have worked well."

During the time Horizon was in discussions with Cascade, Beech Aircraft was a major lender for the smaller carrier and gaining an agreement with Beech was absolutely essential since Beech had financed Cascade's entire fleet, except for the H-S 748. "The debt service on the Hawker 748s was three times what they were worth," McCaw recalls.

"They only had two of the five BAC1-11s flying at the time and the others were being used for parts," he says, recalling the *Argosy* lesson.

Horizon really couldn't get into the position where it would be saddled with all of Cascade's debt. "We couldn't afford to take over their financing as it was fifty percent greater than the value of the equipment," McCaw says. "At the time, Cascade had filed for bankruptcy and we weren't getting very far with their attorneys. So, I set up a meeting with Beech which included their fairly new chairman."

Following their first meeting McCaw believed, *This is one of the most naive persons I have ever met!* With the Beech Starship that was under development at the time, Beech Aircraft's chairman and CEO thought it would make him another Bill Lear of the aircraft world.

The meeting took place at the Beech display in the hall at an industry convention. McCaw initiated the conversation. "We want to work with you guys. We think there is value in keeping Cascade alive. They have good employees and there's a good opportunity, but only if we can work together. Cascade isn't fixable without your cooperation."

For this thing to work, it was recognized, at least on Horizon's part, that certain indebtedness had to be waived for the airplanes to stay flying and the acquisition to be successful.

Without giving what McCaw said any thought, Beech's chairman said, "No, you have to pay us *all* the money."

McCaw was shocked. "You don't understand. Horizon doesn't owe you this money."

Beech's chairman just stared at McCaw who responded, "Don't look at me. This is not *our* problem."

"I will *sue* you," Beech's chairman retorted.

"Sue who?"

"Then, I'll sue Cascade."

"They're in Chapter 11. They're bankrupt. They have no money! You can't sue them when they're in bankruptcy, they're protected by the courts!"

Seeing that this conversation was going nowhere, McCaw looked at Beech's corporate counsel and said, "Explain to your chairman what Chapter 11 means."

The discussion continued for about another hour until McCaw got up and announced: "It is obvious to me that there is no one here who can make a decision. You gentlemen have one week to figure it out before we pull the plug on any further discussion on funding."

McCaw's parting shot was: "You are going to end up with a bunch of used airplanes on your ramp and lose a ton of money. We're here to offer you a solution and we're willing to invest some money along with you to fix the problem."

Beech's chairman had been a former engineer and remained with the company for about another year and a half when the manufacturer wrote off about $800 million on its Starship alone and canceled the program.

McCaw acknowledges that it was both Beech and the U.S. Department of Transportation that were the stumbling blocks for Horizon to try to acquire the Cascade operation.

The DOT was caught up in its own bureaucracy and unable to make a central decision. Beech had financed the BAC1-11s with the result that Cascade's entire fleet was over-financed. Essentially, Horizon would have just as soon the BAC1-11s would have gone into oblivion since they were worth only half of what they were financed for. The DOT had guaranteed the loans on the 748s, financing each at $6.5 to $7.5 million each. And it was still a 48-seat airplane; compared with Horizon's cost of $1 million for a completely refurbished F-27 which would perform the same job as well or better. The 748s were judged to be worth only three to four million each based upon their performance as a new aircraft. What this amounted to was, Cascade had roughly seven times the debt service on an individual airplane than what Horizon had. While Cascade might have had an operating profit with full load factors, with their debt service, there was absolutely no way they could have survived.

Vanguard, the holding company for Cascade, brought suit against Horizon for canceling the deal. Vanguard was a company that had invested a lot of money in treasure hunting. While Cascade could have been considered *fool's gold*, Vanguard was, indeed, into seeking sunken ships. McCaw remembers Kuolt leaving a message one day for Vanguard's CEO that the sunken ship wasn't in the Caribbean but in Spokane.

With better luck beneath the surface than above the clouds, and a few million invested, Vanguard ultimatley made a $110 million find in the sea.

In one of its final acts of desperation, Cascade brought in seasoned airline executive Edward Seabrook Fox, 60, naming him chairman and president, succeeding the son of the founder. "Brook" Fox, as he was better known, tried to rescue the image of the near-defunct carrier by announcing plans for bold new marketing, new destinations and an upgrading of the fleet. None had magic enough to pull Cascade out of its spiral into oblivion.

When Horizon and Cascade initially agreed to pursue merger talks, Pacific Northwest newspapers had a feeding frenzy for the latest information. Speculation ranged from the combination going from the 11th largest regional airline in the country to the 4th, which Horizon later became on its own. Would new cities now get air service for the first time? And what would happen to Cascade's hundreds of employees?

But it was not to be.

"If we could have concluded the acquisition in November 1984 as we had hoped when first entering into the agreement with Cascade's majority shareholder on July 31," Kuolt reflected, "it would have been a different story.

Our intent from the outset was to acquire and operate Cascade as a subsidiary, concentrating on northeastern Washington and western Montana where they had established markets.

"It didn't help either one of us for the Department of Transportation's approval to drag on until the end of January 1985, causing both of our operations to lose money. Cascade was unable to stop the drain on its resources and Horizon's added commitment to support Cascade with its creditors cost us as well."

When the attempt to acquire Cascade was first initiated secrecy was extremely important because, if word had leaked, it would have been a huge employee issue for both companies. Thus, there was a code name within Horizon for Mark Chestnutt. It was "Sally." And phone calls from "Sally" were frequent. What made it so amusing, some suspicioned Milt Kuolt was having an affair with someone with that name.

The impact on Horizon's performance for the year in which discussions with Cascade were being pursued was significant. Kuolt recalls: "I figure it cost us in the neighborhood of $4 million by the time we calculate cash infusion, the obligations to Cascade's owners, plus certain guarantees to creditors."

If there was any benefit from the entire effort for its investment, it was in the smaller markets where both carriers were losing money by sharing too few passengers. Horizon was able to remain and, in many instances, had the opportunity to build the market as well.

Horizon had supported Cascade with around one million dollars in cash to sustain its operation during the talks. But, as negotiations ultimately broke down, the proposed acquisition foundered. By then, Cascade was beyond rescue and Horizon walked. Chestnutt was outraged, claiming that the whole scenario had been a sham to bankrupt his airline. The holding company for Cascade filed suit against Horizon but Cascade was bankrupt long before Horizon became involved. The case was quickly dismissed by the courts. Horizon had to write off its investment.

On reflection, the two carriers were like two kids collaborating on a trip to the movies; one bought the tickets but on the way, the other lost the money for the popcorn.

Financing Through Leasing

The financing of new aircraft needed to be carefully analyzed to determine the true earning power of the equipment. Associated with this were certain tax benefits that could be used or sold to others which could provide windfall opportunities. If a carrier spends its money wisely, it can use any cash realized to upgrade its pilots and acquire spares to bring the aircraft on line.

McCaw says Horizon's competitor never did that. They used any cash gained from leasing for day-to-day operations. "They used this money to pay bills already incurred, which resulted in much higher payments than the aircraft could generate in profits, ultimately resulting in a financial death spiral."

Mel Kays, Horizon's CFO at the time of the acquisition by Alaska, remembers a meeting years before, shortly after the Air Oregon acquisition, with bankers in Portland.

"One of our first meetings was with US Bank. Their banker chewed Milt up and down, pointing out that Horizon was in gross default on its borrowing covenants. We had a particular loan that was collateralized by many of our older aircraft. And the banker was going to call the loan until I explained how the system worked.

"We had an agreement with de Havilland to lease their new Dash 8s. In the process, we were going to trade in all our F-27s, complete with spares, as we took delivery on the new aircraft. In the process, we would receive in the neighborhood of $1.7 million with each new Dash 8. This was necessary for us to acquire the new aircraft and de Havilland, in essence, would take that purchase contract to the bank for financing so they would have operating capital. Horizon simply couldn't carry the risk and cost of selling its used aircraft.

"I explained to the banker that with a couple of million dollars loan, he had $7-$9 million in collateral based upon the contract we have with the manufacturer. With that, he calmed down a bit but our relationship was not quite the same thereafter.

"Horizon's operating capital actually came from a couple of sources. One was from operations. Another was when each new Dash 8 was delivered, de Havilland would pay us cash for our F-27 trade-in. The lion's share of that would go to pay back the line to the bank. Then, when we took delivery of the last new Dash 8, we received a final payment of $1,479,000 for the spares."

On another occasion when Horizon was short in making payroll, Kays received an opportune call from one of the salesmen from Fairchild who sold Horizon the Metroliner IIIs. He asked, "Do you need some money?" *This was like asking an indigent if he wanted a handout.*

To which, Kays replied, "Always." So every time a spare engine would be leased, a finance guy from Fairchild would call Douglas Aircraft's financing arm in Long Beach and make the necessary arrangement. Soon, Horizon would have another cash infusion.

Fairchild had another program called "Customer Integration Support." Every time Horizon would lease a new airplane, Fairchild would kick back a check for $500,000 from the tax benefits. So, literally, leasing airplanes was the way to finance the company.

One year, at about Christmas time, Fairchild had a special deal. Kays was told that if Horizon would lease two airplanes, Horizon could gain $1.5 million in Customer Integration Support. That was too great an inducement to ignore. Kays flew back from Sun Valley between Christmas and the New Year to consummate the deal. $750,000 per aircraft was too good to pass up.

Meeting The Challenges — Turbulence

B ruce McCaw recalls that at SeaTac, when something was wrong with an airplane, Kuolt would have the mechanic on the tarmac explaining to him what was wrong instead of letting the individual go ahead and fix the plane. McCaw reasoned, "Milt, why don't you talk to him after the plane is gone?" Instead, Kuolt would bend the mechanic's ear for twenty minutes, trying to determine just what was wrong and how long it would take and on and on. Kuolt had a "hands on" philosophy that penetrated every department. He was everywhere, confident that his input was needed if everything was going to go right.

"Have you ever talked with anyone who grew up with a big family in a two-room house?" Dee Dee Maul asks. "You know what they say; 'As crowded as it was, it was great!' That was what it was like in the early days of Horizon. Later, we had a *ten-room* house and everybody spread out and everything changed."

"There was magic there in the beginning," recalled Don Welsh. "It was Camelot. Everybody was there for the cause. There was no distinction between management and employees. Then things began to change. Growth began to rob Horizon of its magic and I had come to question my relevance as a manager."

Welsh and Maul were not alone in their concerns. According to other accounts, Milt's micro-management style competed with the decisions of the people he had entrusted with responsibility in the various areas of the growing company. Line management's frustration reached a peak in the fall of 1985 when senior managers rented an airport hotel suite for a three-hour meeting. Kuolt was not invited.

According to some accounts, frustration came to the fore at a senior staff meeting where Milt was very irritable. His irritability was partially due to disappointment with Bob Jorgenson, recently VP of operations. Further, Kuolt felt he, personally, was out of touch and out of control with his senior management.

"It's time you start running this thing – I can't do it all for you," he blurted out. "So, you guys get together and figure out how in the hell you are going to make this thing work!"

Following this little episode, George Bagley and Dee Dee Maul reasoned, "Let's get together off-site and have a planning day and see if we can't do what Kuolt suggested: that is, make this thing work on our own. And, we'll do it without getting Milt involved." Maul bristles at the suggestion that it was a coup. It was just some very dedicated people wanting to make it all come together.

A small conference room was arranged at a hotel near SeaTac. As those involved were getting ready to leave for the meeting, someone asked, "Did we get a flip chart?" Bagley said there was one in Milt's office, but Kuolt was in a meeting. Maul knocked on his door and said she was taking the flip chart for a meeting. Of course, Kuolt asked: "What meeting is that?" To which Maul responded, "Oh, we are all going to get together."

"Oh, are you? Isn't that just great!" It was apparent by Kuolt's tone that he suspected what was going on.

Maul doubts to this day if Kuolt realizes there was no *palace coup.*

"And, what we were doing is exactly what he told us to do in that meeting, which we viewed as an opportunity to get together without him."

McCaw was the senior management person present to help sort it all out. "We were under intense pressure – plus, the company was struggling financially – there were just a lot of things." Everyone was in agreement on one thing and that was Kuolt was being tough on everybody. McCaw told everyone that if they were doing their job, to just continue doing so and ignore Milt, just give it the best shot they could.

"I wasn't trying to do anything differently," McCaw reflects. "I was trying to make his plan work. The outcome was the same; it was just that the path was different. I told them, 'Just don't listen to what he says. Think about what he means.' Kuolt often would be so adamant about something that if you listened to him too carefully, it was going to be a problem."

"There was a lot of emotion and frustration coming to a head," Bill Ayer recalls, "People felt they just had to get away from Kuolt and talk about what was bothering them. My role was to point out that Milt Kuolt is the way he is and he was never going to change. And, we either had to figure out how we were going to deal with that or do something else for a living."

Many say that as a result of that meeting, managers began to more effectively communicate with one another. They affirmed their solidarity and came to an understanding that they were all in the same boat. Managers were hopeful that Kuolt would realize that he had to give up some internal control and bring in a strong operating officer who would assume some of the day-to-day details with which Milt was so burdened. Should that not happen, the managers would prepare for the possibility that Horizon might get a new Chief Operating Officer another way: by being acquired by a larger airline.

"No one ever questioned Kuolt's value to the company," Ayer believes. "Horizon's employees knew they wouldn't have been where they were if it hadn't been for Milt and his style. I mean the growth and good things that happened to Horizon emanated from Milt Kuolt. His style was completely appropriate for the first two or three years. But by later 1985, we were no longer a startup operation, flailing around, trying to find ourselves. We were a major company that needed to be managed."

Kuolt knew it, too. "It was such a damned challenge. We were a teenager trying to be an adult. That's what we were." But, he assured an interviewer from Inc. Magazine in early 1986, "Help is on the way. I plan to add experienced management. Granted, the last time we tried, it didn't work out, but the company now has a stronger personality. An incoming manager won't be so tempted to say, 'This is the way we did it at TWA.' I never gave a damn how they did it at TWA anyway. Besides, now I am more willing to accept help."

F-27s before and after. (Photos courtesy Dick Heaton.)

The Skyjacking

A new and unexpected challenge took place in the skies over Oregon on May 2, 1986 when a Horizon Metroliner was skyjacked by a passenger. Just after 9 p.m., pilot Rick Smith and copilot John McDonald took off from Mahlon Sweet airport in Eugene, Oregon for a regularly scheduled flight to Portland, estimated time of arrival 9:50. Eleven passengers were onboard. No flight attendants were on duty for the popular quick trip, except for one flight attendant who was a non-revenue passenger.

Cruising along, the first indication that this trip would be anything but routine was when one of the passengers, a 29-year-old man from Tulsa, Oklahoma, stood in the aisle and advanced to the flight deck. He knelt down between Smith and McDonald and poked "something" into Rick's ribs, saying, "Head south and keep climbing!" There is no door between the flight deck and the passenger cabin on the Metroliner. Rick described the skyjacker as "a big white male, balding, heavy-set, scraggly looking."

The passengers saw what was happening and remained calm, slightly curious about what the guy was doing out of his seat and on the flight deck. *Horizon passengers showing their cool!* They registered surprise with an unusual calm when they realized the aircraft was approaching Hillsboro instead of going on to Portland. The pilots convinced the skyjacker that if they were to meet his demand to fly to Mexico, they had to stop at Hillsboro, southwest of Portland, to get more fuel.

All passengers were allowed to deplane at Hillsboro and glad to do so. The cabin door was left open to the

18-passenger Metroliner

outside. The skyjacker agreed to allow McDonald to go to the terminal to arrange for refueling and to *call the local FBI office!*

The skyjacker was in the plane with pilot Smith. Fifteen minutes later, the FBI negotiator was on the radio, giving the skyjacker his options. Rick Smith told the skyjacker he had to close the cabin door, which was just a few steps from the cockpit. The skyjacker agreed and just as Rick got to the door, he quickly bolted from the aircraft, leaving the subject alone to ponder his fate. *Surely, he realized that he was not going to Mexico that night.*

After nearly three hours of negotiation, the skyjacker surrendered to authorities. It was 12:50 a.m. He was cuffed and immediately led away.

Dee Dee Maul was home when she got a call from George Bagley "in the middle of the night." The Portland station manager for Horizon was John Chamberlain. He and Dee Dee talked and Chamberlain immediately gathered blankets and assembled a ground crew in vans and headed for Hillsboro to pick up the passengers. The passengers gave high marks to Horizon for the quick resolution to the skyjacking and on how well Horizon treated them after the harrowing incident.

It was learned that later, the skyjacker suffocated himself while in prison.

Three thousand miles away, Bruce McCaw and Tom Cufley were involved in "One Lap of America," otherwise known as a "cannonball run" originating in Detroit, MI. The event was an 8800-mile auto race they completed in eleven days. At McCaw's invitation, Cufley had taken time off from flying for more down-to-earth pursuits in a Mercedes 300E.

They made a brief stop in upstate New York where McCaw spied a headline in the local paper. "Skyjacking!" Looking more closely at the story, he was shocked to see that it was a Horizon plane.

When McCaw told Cufley about the incident, Cufley's immediate reply was, "They what? Milt's gonna *love* that!"

Party Time

Milt Kuolt inspired his employees to serve above and beyond the normal call of duty but he was always ready to provide a party to boost employee spirits. Such special events included flying to destinations such as Reno or Hawaii, or took place under a huge tent in the parking lot at the airline's corporate offices, or at his Spanish-style home overlooking the Puget Sound. Or, on an airplane.

Once Tom Cufley had been in Amsterdam to pick up the second Fokker F-28. He was told by

We're Having
Our 1st
Anniversary Party!

Come join us Wednesday,
September 1, 1982 · 4 PM to 7 PM

Celebrate our first anniversary at
our new Corporate Headquarters.
Corner of South 188th and
Des Moines Way

Fun
Prizes
Open Bar
Hors d'oeuvres

Horizon Airlines, Inc.
26731 - 12th Place South
Seattle, WA 98168
(206) 241-6757

Kuolt to swing by Toronto and pick up about twenty Horizon employees who had been invited by de Havilland for the roll out of the manufacturer's 7,000th airplane, which was being delivered to Horizon. In honor of the city the carrier first served, the new plane was named *"The Great City of Yakima."* Bringing his employees to the rollout was Milt's way of saying thanks for a job well done.

When the cockpit crew came aboard the F-28 the next morning, all twenty were there and the party was well underway. Comparing it with one of Hugh Hefner's Playboy flights might be a stretch but let's just say everyone was having a good time. Except for Cufley and his co-pilot whose job it was to get everyone safely back.

This particular aircraft would be new to the United States. Cufley asked de Havilland if they would file the flight plan and alert U.S. Customs in Buffalo of their pending arrival. "Sure will!" he was assured. It was only about a 15-minute flight across Lake Ontario into Buffalo,

Welcome

de HAVILLAND
A BOEING COMPANY **CANADA**

*The de Havilland Aircraft Company of Canada,
a Boeing Company,
extends a warm welcome to our friends
from Horizon Air
on the occasion of the handover
of your fifth Dash 8 aircraft.*

*We are especially proud that this aircraft,
serial No. 50,
is the 7000th aircraft
manufactured by our Company.*

*We look forward to a continuing successful relationship
between our two companies.*

so no problem, right? Wrong! The folks at de Havilland failed to follow up on Cufley's request so Customs was totally unprepared. This was not a first time experience for Cufley as he had been bringing new Dash-8s through on a regular basis. But the uninformed individuals in the Customs office were angry. Cufley escorted the Customs officer out to the aircraft. Hearing the partying long before he saw it, the official poked his head into the plane's cabin and shook his head. He fined Horizon $2,500 for failure to notify.

On another occasion, en route to Seattle with an F-28, Cufley made a low pass over the main runway in Yakima, not with a slowed approach but at about 300 knots with gear retracted and about fifty feet above the tarmac. It just so happened that an air show was in progress and an FAA official by the name of Bob Norton was present. When Tom landed the F-28, Norton was there to greet him.

"Well, that was interesting, Tom! Want me to put you on the air show waiver?" (A waiver was what pilots of aerobatic aircraft had to have to demonstrate their stunting skills.) Later that day, with a waiver, Tom made another low pass in the F-28. This time without piquing the FAA official.

Fiesta!

Milt Kuolt in his Mexican Generale getup at one of the parties at his home.

Fiestas were a major annual event at the home of Milt and Kathy Kuolt. Complete with live Mariachi bands and a food table that would have satisfied Pancho Villa's army, the evening was festive from start to finish. Fresh margaritas spewed from the fountain on the back lawn as a pet macaw made its presence known, squawking or otherwise entertaining the crowd. Kathy moved among the guests, resplendent in a peasant blouse and skirt or another simple but elegant ensemble, flashing her sweet, sincere and captivating smile. And her partner, Milt, in his Mexican *Generale's* getup made sure every glass was full as he visited with his guests for the evening. The Kuolts invited old friends, new friends, employees of Horizon and Thousand Trails, investors and other business associates. Everyone always had a good time at a fiesta!

Today, the fond memories of fiestas at Milt and Kathy's evoke raw emotional responses. For the people who care about Milt and loved Kathy, they are bittersweet, recalling the camaraderie of the event no one wanted to miss; special times they will never experience again.

The Kuolts gave other fiestas at Elkhorn. One was especially memorable when about nine hundred guests gathered to celebrate the refurbished Elkhorn Lodge and experience the hospitality of Milt and Kathy Kuolt.

Happy Birthday!

On the occasion of Milt's 60th birthday, Kathy secretly chartered one of Horizon's planes and flew into Sun Valley and Elkhorn Resort as many friends, family and associates as the aircraft could carry to the party of parties.

The guest arrival for Milt's 60th birthday party at Sun Valley.

It was during the Elkhorn annual Governor's Cup golf tourney and Milt didn't have an inkling of the surprise. Idaho's Governor Cecil Andrus was in on the surprise and served as honorary host at a banquet for about 400 guests under a tent on the lawn.

The governor took Milt aside asking if they could spend a few minutes away from the gathering. The pair walked across the plaza to the restaurant Milt had built there called Tequila Joe's. Kuolt walked in and saw thirty-five of his and Kathy's close friends.

Milt says he's not "big on surprises" but this one was overwhelming. He was virtually speechless and, for Kuolt, that is something. "Hell, it brought tears to my eyes," he recalls years later.

Dee Dee Maul says that everyone was in the cantina when, on the grassy area outside, a lady rode up on a beautiful horse. They had wanted to do a Lady Godiva-type thing but just couldn't put it all together. But what was done is forever etched on the memories of those who were there. The purebred appaloosa was presented by Joe Clark and Bruce McCaw. The lady dismounted and the rider-less horse was led directly into the restaurant through the back door as the celebrating crowd cheered.

His eyes sparking with excitement and gratitude, still shaking his head in disbelief, Milt mounted up, right there on the restaurant floor and vanished out the same back door. He could have been cast as the hero in a western movie.

Later, someone took a classic photo of Milt on his appaloosa with his friend, Leon Guitterez, similarly attired in hat and duster, riding along on a well-traveled trail with the glorious fall colors of Sun Valley in the background.

Mexico

Milt Kuolt has had a strong affinity for Mexico since first visiting there in the early 1960s. Mostly he journeyed to Puerto Vallarta and Mazatlan, both popular destinations with the old Argosy Travel club. Then, early in the 1990s, he bought a villa at Puerto Vallarta. It was on the 9th fairway at the Los Flamingos Golf Course and was both a birthday and an anniversary gift for Kathy. Milt wasn't fond of his neighbors, a couple that would drink and yell every night. He approached the builder of their house and asked him if he thought the noisy couple would sell. They would and Milt bought the house.

Milt admits that it wasn't exactly a testimony to his good judgment but he got rid of the undesirables that way. In the second house, much to their chagrin, they discovered many *alacranes,* 'scorpions' in English. Kathy coined the name *Casa Alacranes* for the house because it had so many of them. She and Milt agreed that house #5 looked better. And there were fewer scorpions. So they moved into it.

Now with two houses, Milt decided to buy more so he could put together little golf groups as sort of a hobby. Kuolt suggested to Pepe Ramos, owner of the Azteca Restaurant chain, that he should also come down and buy a house. Pepe did.

Milt was now in a house buying frenzy, buying two more houses; sort of a Habitat for Humanity in reverse. He observed that the Mexican builder wasn't doing as well as Milt thought he could, and Milt offered to buy two more uncompleted houses for the price of the lots and partial construction. To these, Milt added another swimming pool that the builder had been unable to complete. There were a total of twenty houses with pools in the development and Kuolt recognized that his investment would be worth more when the project was complete. Now, all the houses were built and all the swimming pools were in. In retrospect he says, "I am not sure I knew what I was doing, but I ended up owning seven villas in the complex."

The builder at Los Flamingos was not the only one to benefit from Milt's investments in Mexico. Early on, when he was CEO of Thousand Trails, he had heard of an orphanage in Mazatlan. It was about Christmas time and Kuolt planned a surprise for those within the company who came down for a big party.

Kuolt decided he would surprise all his guests and not tell them where they were going. Herding all 30 or 40 of them aboard a bus, they drove to *Ciudad de los Ninos*, an orphanage. They arrived in time for the children's Christmas party put on by the nuns and the padre. Actually, it was their idea for Milt to bring his guests along – knowing Milt, he never does anything in a small way.

"I knew they really needed money," Milt explained. " I supported them a little bit and I thought that maybe my guests would want to chip in a little as well." So, Milt asked the sister if she could bring something to gather money in and she brought him a little cup. "No, no, something bigger," he suggested. "We need a bucket!" A bucket was placed right at the front door, but the sisters and padre quickly reminded Milt that the Christmas program was free, that there was no charge. He said, "No, I am going to charge for this so you are not to worry."

The program concluded. As the guests departed, Milt stood by the bucket and each guest started to toss in two, three or five pesos. "No," he announced. "To get into this show costs a lot more than a few pesos so just reach into your pocket and put in twenty, thirty or forty dollars, or, if you have a hundred just sitting idle throw that in the bucket as well."

Several hundred or maybe a thousand dollars were contributed from the group. Milt says the sisters were very embarrassed that he was charging everyone to see the show. However, with the money that was contributed, the orphanage was able to do some things they couldn't have otherwise done for the children.

Coming from India and seeing poverty firsthand as a youth stuck with Milt. He readily recognizes when people need help and that compels him to become involved.

Many years ago in Seattle when two elderly ladies were bilked out of about $4,000 in savings just before the Christmas holidays, the press gave it wide attention. It was a classic "pigeon drop" perpetrated by the lowest form of society. The ladies were devastated – until a check arrived in the mail from a concerned citizen in the exact amount that was stolen from them. The donor insisted on anonymity.

Manufacturers' Mating Dance

So, you think that when you walk into an auto dealership you're getting a fast hustle? Try owning an airline.

Bruce McCaw had made several trips to England's Farnsborough and the Paris Air Shows when the airline was in its early years and had identified many potential suppliers and manufacturers as candidates to upgrade Horizon's future fleet.

It was time. With various types of aircraft, if something was broken, it needed a different box of parts. To top it all off, the FAA was climbing Horizon's frame. The primary concern was the carrier's old airplanes. Plus, there was a higher than usual number of cancellations.

Heading the list of courtesans was de Havilland of Canada. Horizon had been working on a contract to acquire the manufacturer's Dash 8 aircraft for about a year and a half. Horizon's board had already approved the purchase.

About nine o'clock one evening, Duncan MacIntyre of de Havilland and Bruce McCaw had reached a point of agreement for the purchase. No more negotiating. Bruce signed the contract with a gold Cross pen, presented for the occasion, and put it into his pocket. The next day he and Duncan had an audience with Milt.

"Milt comes into the meeting screaming at Duncan," McCaw recalls, "and says, 'We're not going to do this! We're not going to buy these airplanes unless you do this and this...' Duncan was ready to faint."

McCaw stayed calm and when Milt was finished, said, "Hey, Milt, it's done and signed and we got a good deal. So, that's it." Milt didn't say another word. McCaw didn't have to say anything more. Theirs is a wonderful two-way working relationship, with mutual respect for each other.

Kuolt recalls that every Dash 8 amounted to about a six million-dollar purchase. "We don't have any money," Kuolt told the de Havilland sales team. "So, you'll have to take our F-27s in trade." He said that over time it would have involved about ten F-27s. "So, if we can lease the planes for $40,000 a month, then you have a deal!" de Havilland took Horizon's aging F-27s in trade. It ended up being a more costly deal than the Canadian manufacturer had bargained for. Horizon, though, had options for ten more aircraft.

In retrospect, it is recognized by those involved that Horizon had cut a Sweetheart Deal. It was a good deal for de Havilland as well because, since the initial program launching the Dash 8, the manufacturer had not sold a single plane to a major fleet customer or to any airline on the West Coast.

The marketplace for 40-seat aircraft was very competitive between the French ATR, the Dutch Fokker F-27, the Casa 235, the Spanish/Indonesian consortium, Brazil's Brazilia and the Canadian Dash 8.

In 2001, Horizon was taking delivery of CRJ-700s from Bombardier, the successor to de Havilland. The plane is a 70-seat jet replacing the airline's Fokker F-28s and is receiving excellent passenger acceptance.

McCaw saw MacIntyre again about a year after the Alaska acquisition and was told that Alaska was thinking about canceling the balance of the options to get some money back. McCaw was appalled as Horizon had got "one hell of a deal on the options."

McCaw convinced John Kehoe, Horizon's VP of finance, Art Thomas, general counsel, and VP of operations George Bagley that they should hold on to the options. They did and it ultimately saved Horizon about eight million dollars in the purchase of future aircraft, or in option sales.

Horizon had studied aircraft acquisition as thoroughly as it could have been studied. It is always a bit of a crap shoot when a carrier buys a new airplane, but Horizon was convinced the Dash 8 was the best airplane for its time. The carrier had great confidence in de Havilland's management and their honest dealings with them.

McCaw observes that the "worst thing" for de Havilland was when Boeing bought them, later selling the Canadian manufacturer to Bombardier. Despite de Havilland's great history both in Canada as well as the UK, it was a classic culture clash. "Boeing is a superb company," McCaw says, "but you can't run something the size of de Havilland the same way you run Boeing."

Milt went to Brazil at the invitation of Colonel Ozires de Silva, chairman of Embrarer, a South American manufacturer of the Brazilia, a 30-passenger aircraft, compared to the 37-passenger Dash 8. Milt says de Silva is "probably one of the finest gentlemen I have ever met."

He escorted Milt and Kidwell through his factory, following which Milt thought very favorably about doing a deal with Embrarer. The clincher for de Havilland, however, was its greater cargo capacity and its 37 seats versus 30 on the Brazilia. Plus the faster Embrarer aircraft lacked the necessary takeoff and landing characteristics to fly the microwave landing system planned for Sun Valley.

Horizon also talked with the French manufacturer Aerospatiale in Toulouse. The French were very interested in selling Horizon their ATR-42 aircraft. First, at the Paris Air Show, Kuolt and McCaw met with Henri Puell, who was then number two person with that aircraft's program. They met twice again, at Horizon's Seattle offices and in the Caribbean at a Regional Aircraft Association conference.

The French were insistent that for any aircraft acquisition, there must be a down payment. Remember, this was when Horizon was struggling financially and Kuolt's personal assets were on the line to keep Horizon flying. During one discussion in Horizon's home office, talks came to such a point of frustration, that Milt Kuolt was literally stacking some of the gold bars he owned personally on the table, plus offering a free and clear title to his recently-constructed Spanish-style home overlooking the waters of Puget Sound. None of this seemed to satisfy the Frenchmen's demand for down payment. Kuolt upped the ante by adding the soon to be built Horizon corporate headquarters building *and* his house! But, as he says today, "They didn't want any mortgages."

At the RAA conference in the Caribbean, Henri Puell and Kuolt again went around and around and McCaw remembers the Frenchman had literally chewed his cigar to a frazzle. Milt was having fun. Henri was perplexed. Obviously, he had never met anyone like Milt Kuolt

"The *frogs* had some pretty nice guys," Kuolt reflects, "but they were a real arrogant bunch, talking as if they had the market cornered." *At that time, the book on political correctness had yet to be written.* "I told them, 'Look, I don't give a damn what you have sold, I want an airplane that will suit our operations.'"

Time for McCaw to reenter the discussion as he was the person who did the final evaluation on any airplanes. He and Milt returned to Toronto.

The overall characteristics of the Dash 8 won the sale for the Canadian firm. Although only slightly slower, its cabin was more spacious, it had shorter takeoff and landing characteristics and Horizon's team believed it was quieter. Since Horizon's flight segments averaged about 45 minutes to an hour, speed was not a factor.

In the end, the French ATR couldn't meet its performance guarantees and ended up with other significant shortcomings.

Stock Options and Warrants

The airline industry was capital intensive long before Milt Kuolt decided to take the plunge. Two to three years before Horizon's Initial Public Offering, employees were granted, and exercised options under Incentive Stock Option plans effective in 1981 and 1982. Those options were at $3.00 to $6.00 per share and the number of shares exercisable at December 31, 1985 amounted to 68,150. The company also granted 34,000 options outside the Plan.

Former stockholders of Air Oregon, Inc. in 1982 were issued warrants to purchase 250,000 shares of Horizon common stock at $3.00 per share. In conjunction with the Company's IPO in 1984, the underwriters received warrants to purchase 75,000 of the company's shares at $6.60 per share.

At the end of Fiscal 1985 none of these had been exercised. All unexercised warrants, of course, were dealt with when Alaska later acquired Horizon at $9.50 per share.

Enter the investment bankers.

There are bankers and then there are investment bankers. You meet them when planning an Initial Public Offering and at any subsequent financing along the way – again when selling a company. As one disgruntled seller of a company put it, "they are underwriters going in and undertakers going out."

The "dog and pony show" is part of the program in corporate finance. Hat in hand, the underwriter leads you to those who are going to sell your stock, hopeful that you'll do a good enough job that they may even be able to peddle the over allotment, equal to ten percent over the number of shares in the Initial Public Offering. Kuolt's hat wasn't exactly in his hand that cold day in January 1984 when he marched into the Denver offices of Boettcher & Co, his underwriter. In fact, his hat was on his head, a Goofy cap such as one would see kids wearing at Disneyland. You know the one, with the bill of the cap forming Goofy's snout and the long dog ears covering yours. Those present glanced at each other and mumbled nearly incoherent mutterings like, "If you say so."

That was and is Milt Kuolt. Why not? The world of corporate finance is replete with Stetsons, beanies, turbans, yarmulkes and, some say, more often than not, dunce caps. Certainly the audience of pinstripes and paisley suspenders was prepared for the usual presentation of tiresome slides and palaver, their anticipated anguish mellowed somewhat by the promise of a free lunch. But they soon learned from whence Kuolt was coming. His disdain for the conventional flew in the face of the traditional sucking up to those who were to peddle your stock. From the time he entered the dining area of Denver's Brown Palace Hotel, in his Goofy Hat, where he almost knocked over the dessert cart, promoting someone to whisper, *"That's nothing! You ought to see him in a china shop,"* Kuolt had his audience sitting up and asking for more.

When the *dog* was back in its kennel and the *pony* out to pasture, the brokers and security analysts present were sold. Horizon's stock came to market on January 25, 1984 at $5.50 a share, with nearly $4 million net to the airline after underwriting commissions.

Mark Vander Ploeg, who headed up the Boettcher offering, said he had no trouble putting together the underwriting group but it was not an easy sell all the way through. "The greatest obstacle was starting an airline from scratch. Another was the poor track record of other airlines that were struggling." Yet another problem for the underwriter was that investors look hard at the experience of management. While Kuolt had no previous airline experience, as a true entrepreneur, he did have the success of Thousand Trails behind him that really helped. Vander Ploeg remembers the road show experience: "It was a meeting prospective investors will never forget, nor would Boettcher partners."

Immediately following the IPO, the stock began to sag and Boettcher had to support the after market. Somewhat like flying a plane, the stock went up and down, with occasional turbulence.

For security analysts it was not the run of the mill interview when visiting Milt Kuolt at Horizon. His candor was refreshing, although at times startling.

Bill Whitlow, now with Safeco's Northwest Fund, was with the Seattle brokerage firm Dain Bosworth when Horizon went public. After meeting with Mike Lowry, Whitlow was directed to Kuolt's office to continue the meeting. *It must have been one of the times when the red flag should have been out.* Kuolt's opener was " I don't want to talk with any more (expletive) security analysts." One can assume that previously other analysts had not been too kind when describing the carrier's financial condition.

Once the "introduction" was out of the way, they went on to have a good interchange.

Subsequent Financing

A successful IPO doesn't mean an end to the search for capital. Along the way the company had authorized 5,000,000 shares of preferred stock. However, none were outstanding as of the June 4, 1985 when Boettcher & Co. and Piper Jaffray and Hopwood co-managed a 1,100,000-share offering of "$1.20 Cumulative Convertible Exchangeable Preferred Stock." No attempt will be made here to describe the details of such an instrument other than to say, it could be converted at any time into Common Stock at $7.70 per share "subject to adjustment in certain events." After underwriting commissions Horizon netted $10,147,500 the proceeds of which were to be used "to pay trade payables, to repay certain borrowings and provide working capital."

By February 12, 1986 when Mark Vander Ploeg became

affiliated with E.F. Hutton, a multi-faceted plan was presented to Horizon ranging from financial restructuring to the outright sale of the airline. One of the paramount concerns stated by Hutton was dealing with the preferred shareholders: "Unless profitability can be achieved promptly, the Board will be forced to address the question of Horizon's ability to continue to pay preferred dividends *(quarterly, at a rate equivalent to 12% a year)*. Discontinuing the preferred dividends would sharply affect the market value of both the preferred and common stock, which ultimately would adversely impact both Horizon's and Milt Kuolt's commercial banking relationships."

Really? Well, Kuolt had been here before. Only, this time, as founder and major shareholder, his personal financial situation was heavily dependent upon Horizon's success. Also, his position as guarantor on certain commercial bank loans to Horizon had to be addressed for his as well as Horizon's future.

E.F. Hutton served as investment bankers to the airline industry. Since 1979, the firm had completed over 80 investment banking assignments for over 20 airline industry clients. Being blunt was the due diligence part of the game.

Hutton was engaged for the assignment that required an initial retainer and a success fee related to the size of the transaction. The retainer to be credited against any success fee.

Code Sharing

I n the summer of 1985, Horizon had entered into an agreement with United Airlines to share their two-letter airline code (UA). A person booking a flight from Chicago to Yakima, for example, would buy a ticket that showed United service all the way. In reality, however, it would be service on a Horizon aircraft for the last leg between Seattle and Yakima. This arrangement was intended to simplify ticketing between the two airlines but Horizon management failed to see the benefit to their airline.

Horizon knew it was critical to maintain its own identity but since the relationship between Milt and United was like trying to mix water and oil, a change in procedure would be difficult. One of the sticking points was the question of how to negotiate a formula for incremental traffic, no small potatoes to Horizon. Through code sharing, United was realizing about

$135 per passenger and there were ten thousand passengers a month. Horizon wasn't getting anything back. By analyzing traffic data, it was apparent there was an immediate shift from Alaska and other carriers to United. Right up until the day the deal with Alaska was finalized, Horizon continued to try to negotiate better terms with United.

There would have been less pressure for Horizon to sell to Alaska if United had been more cooperative in giving Horizon the cost-revenue sharing it needed. McCaw was quick to convey his concerns that a total trip identity as "United" would "destroy" Horizon.

Kuolt wanted the code sharing arrangement with United to work and, while continuing to negotiate with United, Kuolt initially threw cold water on any talk about cutting a deal with Alaska, despite a visit from Gus Robinson, then president of Alaska Airlines.

"He was a gruff old guy and came in here and started throwing out a lot of numbers," Kuolt said. "I asked him, 'what in the hell are you talking about? We have an arrangement for code sharing with United.' I was feeling pretty bullish."

Milt was confident that a deal might ultimately be done with United, so he was dealing from a comfortable position. Milt believes that the knowledge of Horizon's arrangement with United was what really prompted Alaska to take a heightened interest in his airline.

Kuolt kept reminding Robinson of the United agreement, saying, "We'll probably do a deal with them." That seemed to whet Alaska's appetite for the regional even more. However, after two or three meetings with Robinson, Kuolt couldn't handle it any more and told Alaska to "just forget it."

In a recent interview, Bruce Kennedy, now an Alaska director and chairman of its executive committee, agreed. "We felt that Horizon's effort at code sharing with United was a key motivator that drove us to discussions."

So the conversation continued. Kuolt, Robinson and Kennedy had lunch at SeaTac's Red Lion to discuss issues of mutual interest. Despite strong emotions on either side of Pacific Highway South, Bruce McCaw and Ray Vecci of

Alaska became good friends. One night they met for five hours just to discuss where each side was and what it would take to do a deal.

Robinson retired from Alaska while discussions were still in progress. Shortly thereafter, Vecci who, at the time was Alaska's Vice President of Planning, came back to Kuolt saying that Alaska would like to continue discussions. "By the way," Kuolt says now, "down deep in my belly, I was pretty excited about having a suitor for our airline.

"I remember Vecci. I really liked him but I was sticking with the $12 a share asking price when our stock was trading around 5-1/2."

Ray remembers Milt calling him during this period with a specific question about "traffic" to which Vecci responded, "I don't know." In typical fashion, Kuolt retorted, "If I had a person with your responsibility who didn't have an answer to *that* question, I'd fire him." A year later in Sun Valley, relaxing over drinks, Ray asked Milt, "Do you remember when you fired me?" Kuolt didn't.

The ball was handed off to Bruce Kennedy. Kuolt says, "I used to call him the 'Hallelujah Kid' and the rest of the Alaska hierarchy the 'Boutique Chocolatiers.' Bruce Kennedy was truly a quality person. Alaska was a well-run company with some good people."

The Alaska negotiating team also had their opinions of Kuolt which included the "Shoot From the Lip Maverick" and "Uncle Miltie," referring to legendary comedian, Milton Berle. But, if any deal was to be done, they were all to be discreet enough to keep their impressions to themselves.

Regarding the makeup of Alaska's board of directors at the time, Kennedy says, "I have always felt that one of our strengths was that we didn't have professional directors; that the people on our board had a real passion for our airline and the people we serve. Once the makeup of our board was explained to Peter Lynch, a recognized financial guru, now heading up Fidelity Investments, he understood their diverse backgrounds and accepted the board for what it was."

As for Kuolt, he reflects, "I had the best damn board that anybody could have in their company. These guys were outspoken. They had their opinions. I had a high respect for all of them and they helped me a lot."

Alaska Acquires Horizon

In recounting the Horizon acquisition by Alaska, it is important to point out the members of Kuolt's auspicious board. They included Bruce McCaw; Frank Bryant with Bateman Eichler, an investment banking firm; Andy Andersen, formerly of the Air Oregon board; Bob Brazier, president of Airborne Express; Bruce Johnson, CEO of Geosafe Corporation; and Mark Vander Ploeg, of E.F. Hutton.

Kuolt especially remembers Andy Andersen when he had to muster the Horizon board prior to the Alaska acquisition, during a critical time for cash flow. "I guess you guys know I need your help – and here's the deal. I have payroll coming up in about six days, plus airplane payments. I am short on cash – and I mean *really* short. Someone on the board asked 'how short?' I told them 'we need a million bucks!'"

Kuolt watched his board. Each man was looking pensively out the window. There was no response. Andy Andersen went from face to face, watching for a glimmer of hope; something, anything at all. He glanced over at his friend, Milt Kuolt, whose expression was a mix of anticipation and desperation. Finally, Andy broke the silence.

"Talk to my guy in Portland and I'll have a million for you tomorrow."

"Andy bailed us out of this big, dark, black hole," Kuolt recalls. "We paid Andy back and then some. I guess he didn't want to have an airplane back in his lap – I just don't know. But, he's the guy who stepped up with just a handshake and we drew up a couple documents and he came up with the cash."

Kuolt acknowledges that Horizon hadn't been performing that well and that his carrier needed more mature management.

"I knew it was time for me to get the hell out and get some real good operators; some more seasoned management in there."

Kennedy recognized that Kuolt had done a good job with Thousand Trails, and had been successful in building Horizon into a very successful regional and remembers he said at the time, "Milt should take our cash offer now and let us run with it. We were prepared to take over his legacy."

Mark Vander Ploeg was present in New York with Kuolt in January of 1987 when Alaska Air Group was about to consummate its purchase of Horizon Air. Alaska, at the time, was recovering from a short strike by flight attendants and was seeking to recover some of their lost traffic.

There were those within Horizon who just didn't want the company sold. Bruce McCaw was one of them. When it came down to the vote, McCaw was the only Horizon board member opposed to the sale. For him, it was a matter of principle. He hated to sell the airline but knew that if such a deal was in the offing, it should be to Alaska. When it was all over, he agreed that the price paid was fair.

Vander Ploeg, also a Horizon director and with E.F. Hutton at the time, believes that the $9.50 a share negotiated for each Horizon outstanding share was the best Horizon could expect. He recalls telling Horizon's board that Alaska's offer was one they could feel free to accept. The transaction totaled nearly $70 million of which Kuolt received about $26 million for his shares.

The only pressure to hurry the transaction was to complete an agreement before the 1986 year ended when tax consequences would have been much greater for the selling shareholders.

It has been said that within months after the acquisition, someone at Alaska remarked that they could have paid 50 percent more for the airline and it still would have been a good deal. Of course, with hindsight, no one really knew what the fairest price should have been. Kuolt says that he had to convince Kennedy to even come up with the $9.50 a share, which was more than a 70 percent premium over where Horizon's stock had been trading.

Some believe there were certain items Horizon could have negotiated harder and not all were financial. The acquisition of Horizon has proved to be a boon for Alaska. But there was always the outside chance that Horizon might not have made it had the carrier not been acquired. Even on the day the deal was signed with Alaska, Horizon had some significant financial problems; later with write-offs greater than anyone may have realized.

Yes, there were some surprises but there was no attempt to mislead Alaska at any time along the way. Some of the write-offs were attributable to differences between the two carriers on how certain tangibles, such as aircraft parts, were accounted for.

"Before the first year in the Alaska fold was over, there was some pained discontent." McCaw recalls. "There were some early problems with the de Havilland Dash 8s and some write-offs on the F-27s, but for any surprises Alaska got, they still came out way ahead on the deal. As I look back on it, while initially non-supportive of the sale, I think it was the right thing to do."

The pending close of the Horizon acquisition by Alaska was met with mixed feelings throughout the organization. John Kuolt, from his marketing vantage point, was somewhat disappointed knowing that he likely would be leaving the company he helped build, but pleased with the knowledge that being targeted was recognition that his airline was a valued entity.

John Kuolt recalls that he is the person who hired Bill Ayer who is now the president of Alaska Airlines. George Bagley, who came in with the Transwestern

acquisition, added a lot to the stature of the airline, rising from VP of Operations and now President and CEO of Horizon.

John Kelly

In July 1987, following the acquisition early in the year, John Kelly of Alaska came across the street to become president of Horizon. John Kuolt recalls that Kelly questioned why Horizon was putting so many resources into the Portland market. Coming from an established airline, he had to be reminded that it was Horizon that built the Seattle-Portland route segment. And, it was Horizon that introduced the very popular "a flight every thirty minutes."

If a passenger was late for an 8 o'clock flight, arriving at the gate at 8:05, he had only to wait about another twenty minutes to board the next Horizon flight leaving at 8:30. That service really established Horizon in the eyes of its public. The carrier, recognizing that its biggest competitor was the car, utilized radio advertising to get the message across. It worked. And worked well. At the outset, it was a concept Alaska was slow to understand.

Redmond, Oregon was another of the markets where Horizon's greatest competition was the car. The city fathers had all sorts of wild ideas on air service to their city, including once-a-day flights to San Francisco. Or, starting their own airline. At one point, they even tried to encourage a carrier other than Horizon to serve the city, thinking they could support service greater than Horizon initially planned. Since no other carrier served, or wanted to serve Redmond, it came to some down to earth marketing. John Kuolt and his sales team descended upon the city with their Speed Ticket books. That was a significant inducement for people to begin flying to Portland.

Kelly of Alaska questioned Horizon's speed ticketing. Horizon was the carrier that developed the speed ticketing concept and Alaska couldn't understand why books of tickets were being sold in the Redmond-Portland markets when Horizon was the only carrier flying that city pair. Kelly was again reminded that the competition wasn't another airline but the automobile. With speed ticketing, passengers had the incentive to leave their car and catch the next flight out.

Along with this, arrangements were made with Budget Car Rentals to give a customer the second day care rental free with the first. For the business flier it indeed was an incentive to fly and rent at their destination.

Today Kennedy says that Horizon was a "great proving ground for some of our people such as John Kelly, who followed Milt as CEO and is now Alaska's CEO; and Bill Ayer, who is now president of Alaska."

Ray Vecci is now executive vice president, customer service and president, Michigan operations for Northwest Airlines. He says, "Today a regional carrier might find it more difficult to start up without an arrangement with a major carrier at the outset. In 1981, Alaska's fleet consisted of less than a dozen planes, so it was a period of growth for both carriers."

Recalling Alaska's negotiations with Horizon, Vecci says that it was important to recognize the value of Horizon's management team.

When the acquisition was in its final stages of negotiation, the subject of commissions to be paid to the investment bankers came up. Anyone who has gone through this exercise realizes that the fuzzy-faced young MBAs didn't spend their money at Harvard or Wharton to work for peanuts. In fact, it seemed a little incongruous that two companies, located across the street from one another, had to go to New York to negotiate a deal. But, Alaska needed seventy million bucks and New York was where the money was. Milt was not bashful about giving his opinion on how outrageous he thought the investment bankers' commissions were for doing so apparently little to earn them. No doubt his expressed opinions were the subject of discussion at several Wall Street luncheons for days thereafter.

Comparing commercial bankers with investment bankers, Kuolt believes, "Investment bankers generally have ideas closer to being correct." And he adds, "They are halfway where they should be. The investment banker has to do the right thing. He wants to get to know me and does his due diligence. Often the people they send in to do their due diligence aren't smart enough to know what they are looking at. But at least they get off their asses and into the company where the commercial banker rarely ventures."

As quick as Kuolt can be to offer his perceptions of others, he is equally quick to acknowledge his own weaknesses, especially the difference between his leadership and his management.

"I would say my management techniques are not that good. I think I had some strong leadership qualities that kept the airline glued together over some very difficult times. But, as a manager, I overstepped my bounds way too much. However, I worked especially hard with the rank and file and those at the entry level of the company. I was much easier on them than I was my senior staff who I told, 'You are getting paid a lot more than these people, so get off your asses and go work with them.' And, when they didn't do it, I did it for them."

(Photo courtesy of Ron Suttell)

A Good Deal

The amalgamation with Alaska made a great deal of sense. Both carriers were situated close by one another and their route structures were very complimentary. Horizon's culture did not disappear in the transaction.

The Alaska Air Group decided that both carriers would maintain their separate identity, each with its own management. Horizon did, however, acquire Alaska's "AS" designator and joined its reservations system beginning March 1, 1987. Almost overnight, Alaska realized a significant increase in traffic.

At the time of Alaska Air Group's acquisition, Kuolt indicated his intention to step down as chairman of Horizon but agreed to stay on as a consultant. Executive VP George Bagley acted as the carrier's chief executive officer until June 1987 when John Kelly was elected president and CEO.

Kelly, 43, had some big shoes to fill. But he brought with him twenty years of airline experience with the parent company where he had been a vice president. Kuolt

Bruce Kennedy, Chairman and CEO of Alaska Airlines at the time of the acquisition of Horizon in 1987.

became vice chairman of the board and Bagley remained executive VP and chief operating officer.

A good deal for Alaska. For Horizon, the end of an era. And, the magic continues.

ℛeflections

Bill Peare, who came aboard in 1985 as senior VP of operations, offers his perspective on Horizon Air:

"I have met a lot of very senior people over the years, but I don't know of anyone else who could've pulled off Horizon other than Milt Kuolt. It took his kind of focus, persistence and dedication

Bill Peare

and the ability to attract the right people. Horizon had an awful lot of very, very good people.

"The airline business is a business committed to mistakes. It is the only business where one can get up every day realizing that the roof could fall in with such things as weather, mechanical problems, people. You hope your people get up feeling good, that the passengers get there and that you are able to perform. There are lots of things you can't control.

"I heard a guy say once, 'in the airline business, we train to the highest level of stress.' That's what we tried to bring into the picture with our interviews with customer service reps. We'd ask, 'what keeps you awake nights?' And they'd say 'overbooking.' Okay, let's train to that. We'd ask flight attendants about their greatest level of stress and they'd say 'plane emergencies.' We'd train to that. It's the only industry I know where you have to do that if you're going to be successful.

"Airlines need to do a better job of serving the customer today. I wish the industry could afford to have a back up, spare plane available where you could plug it into the schedule if one has a mechanical or some other problem. Apparently, carriers can't afford to have reserve airplanes around the country that could be ready in an hour. People can understand an hour. You take four, six or eight hours or more, that's ridiculous."

Of course, reflecting on the sale of Horizon, there were questions and some doubts about the transaction. Don Welsh, for example, expressed disappointment when Horizon was sold to Alaska. Although, he says, that the older he gets, the more he recognizes that Milt was wise to understand that there are entrepreneurs whose mission is to *start* businesses and who later realize there are others better suited to take them to the next level. Welsh remembers several distinct highlights in his career with Horizon. One was the first day of service between Seattle and Yakima, another was when the airline went public and the third was the acquisition of Air Oregon and domination over Cascade.

"Horizon redefined what a regional airline should be. Our innovations were much greater than we realized at the time."

A marketing man at heart, Welsh believes that Horizon was the right airline for its time.

"Service is not what drives many airlines today. For Horizon, however, it's still getting a person from Point A to Point B with superb service. The services we initiated at reservations, ticket counters and on our airplanes, made the difference."

Welsh has an extra measure of praise for Kathy Anderson Kuolt and many of the original flight attendants who set the tone for passenger acceptance.

Horizon board member, Bruce Johnson reflects that prior to the meeting at which it was decided to sell Horizon to Alaska, several board members made it clear that, while good arguments *might* be made for not selling the company, the fact that Milt really wanted to do the deal made any argument moot.

Johnson says, "The continuation of Horizon as an independent entity would have required Milt's full time dedication and focus and he seemed anxious to move on to new challenges. He had negotiated what seemed to be a very good deal for the shareholders and had a management team in place with which Alaska seemed satisfied. From an outside director's perspective, it looked very much like a done deal and a deal well done.

"On reflection, it is clear that Milt Kuolt is a builder much more than an operator. Had the Alaska deal not been struck, the Company could have operated for a while without a senior owner or partner but the large scale economics of airline operations would, sooner or later, have put new owners or partners in place. So, Milt got out at the right time. He did a great job of involving his Board. He gave us the data and the information we needed and listened to us as a Board and as individuals."

Mel Kays, although not part of Horizon's founding group, was there as CFO when the airline was sold. He, too, shares the same views as others relative to the

Mel Kays

inequitable code-sharing relationship with United. Kays says that Horizon was able to prove that United was garnering around 60 percent of all interline traffic.

"We demonstrated to United by schedules and projections that we should receive five to six million dollars a year as the result of benefits they were getting from code sharing," Kays says.

The Air Academy

Dee Dee Maul had just gotten the Horizon Air Training Academy under way when the Alaska acquisition took place.

"The Academy had been discussed for months," Kuolt said. "Several people had expressed agreement that we should start it. Bill Peare came to me to urge that we get it rolling and he worked hard to make it a reality."

Ray Hall had taken over the responsibility as director of station operations and Maul was named VP, training and academy development.

"When negotiations with Alaska began, the academy was well under way and it was fabulous!" Maul says today. "The academy, a place for professional training of airline employees, was created with all the right concepts and people were raving about it. I remember when Milt brought Bruce Kennedy of Alaska through, Milt expressed to him that it could be a separate profit center for Alaska." But it wasn't to be. Kennedy told Kuolt that Alaska didn't want to be in the training business.

"I was very hurt and disappointed because I was so excited and motivated and then the whole operation was abruptly terminated," Maul laments. "When this happened, George Bagley said I could have my old job back as VP of station operations. I had mixed feelings because I didn't want to bump Ray Hall out of his newly appointed position. When I discussed this with Milt, he just said 'If I were you, I would just get out.' That's what I did.

"I regret leaving the company when I did. I felt that in assuming my former position, I was taking a step backward."

Maul admits that was an immature rationale. She had grown with the industry and the company, advancing with the academy responsibility. The acquisition by Alaska was untimely for her and she wishes it hadn't happened when it did. But she took Kuolt's advice and left, especially following his suggestion, "When you go, just go quickly." She took this to mean no long good-byes. She also was concerned that some might perceive that she had been asked to leave when she hadn't, at least not directly.

This is the one piece of Milt's advice that she says she has always regretted. Many co-workers, of course, had tremendous respect for Dee Dee. It was a sad departure for all.

As for the training academy, Maul says that their program was just beginning to receive interest from other airlines, which would have used the program initiated by Horizon. Momentum was building to extend the academy beyond just their carrier's station operations, flight attendant and reservations training. Plans also were in the hopper to initiate a training segment on weather.

It was a time when airlines were searching for qualified people and little, if any, training was being offered. All in all, the decision against fulfilling the academy's promise was a great disappointment to Dee Dee Maul.

Bill Peare echoes Maul's sentiments:

"I felt the Air Academy was a milestone in the company's growth and one of its better ideas," Peare recalls. "At the time, I thought our hiring practices were pretty poor in areas such as customer service agents and ramp operations. There were schools out there, supposedly training people in such operations, but I never felt they focused on the appropriate areas. Secondly, we would take almost anybody that we could get.

"The academy was good as a separate profit center. I saw no logic in outsiders training airline personnel when the airline knows what they want. We could basically take the same things and do a better job of training. It would enable us to take the cream of the crop as we were looking at the grades every day. It was our airline people training, so they had their eye out for the best. I think it would have been a home run."

Thoughts from the Chief

There are great men of commerce and industry whose thoughts and sayings are so profound they are recorded for future generations. Any fledgling entrepreneur who dreams big dreams or an executive who might feel like he or she is stagnating, will benefit from what follows in the words of Milt Kuolt:

I am a great admirer of people like Tom Peters who authored *In Search of Excellence*. I like people who dared to be different such as Herb Kelleher of Southwest Airlines.

First of all, the customer, in my view, is always right. I would tell my employees that even when a customer is wrong. And there is a certain manner in which to dialog with them when there is a difference of opinion.

Now, we know that the customer isn't always right, but you have to treat them as if they were in order to resolve any differences.

However, on the flip side, I would never allow any passenger or customer to verbally abuse an employee, particularly a station agent. Which brings to mind the time when I was number four in line while traveling the system. At the counter there was a passenger just raising hell and being very verbally abusive to our person there. She was trying to explain why his bags were lost. He had connected from another airline in Salt Lake City and his bags didn't make our flight. The time was just too short for the connection to be made. He was just raising hell and I heard him shout: "I'm going to talk to your president!"

So, I stepped to the front of the line and tapped him on the shoulder and said, "I guess you want to talk to me." Suddenly, his manner subdued. I told him to leave the counter and that he was never to fly on our airline again. If he wanted, he could rent a car, take a bus, charter a plane,

or even ride a horse. But he was never going to speak to another Horizon employee that way again.

About two months later he wrote me a two-page letter (maybe because he was saddle-sore) and was very apologetic, saying that he realized he shouldn't have spoken so harshly with our station agent. Then, he asked if I would lift the ban on him flying Horizon. Being the *compassionate* person that I am, I agreed. We never heard from him again and, as far as I know, he's still flying Horizon.

About six months before Horizon's first flight in 1981, it came to me that talk on the street was that "Milt will never get his airline off the ground." Further, "he won't even get a certificate and in this environment with interest rates around 18 percent, he'll never get financing." It was kind of upsetting when I heard that people believed I wouldn't be able to pull this thing off. But, we did, and we did very well. You have to ignore what other people say and get on with business.

I had always heard that "patience is a virtue." I guess I have never really understood that. There are times, I guess, when it could be a virtue. But, I for one, am monumentally impatient, always wanting things done now, and not wanting to wait. I could never understand why something would take two days to be accomplished when, in reality, it could be done in 15 minutes. I deplore procrastination and never understood it – and broken promises just don't work with me.

If I asked someone to have a report to me by four o'clock and they would respond: "Well, I'll try…" I would tell them, "Don't try; just do it!" I have no patience with someone who will *just try*. Now, obviously, if someone couldn't make the deadline and then would say, "I tried," I was a bit more tolerant.

When a person would say they would do something, I accepted that the same as if it was a signed contract. And, I just would not accept excuses.

Bureaucracy? I have a profound disgust for it and tried to tear it down in the company when I saw little empires beginning to emerge. The problem with that was that a person would be separating themselves from the team. I would spot that quickly. For example, I remember when I hired a person to head up Human Resources. He asked, "What is my title?" And, I said, "What do *you* think it should be?" He said that it should be director of Human Resources. I responded, "You really mean personnel clerk, don't you?" He countered, "Well, it's a bit more than *that*." "Well," I said, "you are going to be the personnel clerk."

I wasn't big on titles, feeling that people who had them were more obsessed with that than getting their job done. You could go into so many offices of our company, or any company, and the first thing you would see was a little holder with their business cards exhibiting their title. Well, I am not big on that one, either.

On another matter – policies and procedures. When someone tells me, "That's the policy" and I don't think it fits the situation, I tell them, "Change your damn policy! Don't lay your policies and procedures on me!" I know that some policies and procedures are necessary, but, policies and procedures cannot run the company; at least not in an entrepreneurial company. I don't like people to mince their words. I want them to tell it the way it is. That's what's needed when starting any young company – and that's straight shooters; those who won't mince words but will deal with reality.

I was on the board of a company that included two people in the hotel business, another in the restaurant business and me in the airline business. I used to hear how tough all these businesses are. Well, I finally figured out what really is tough and what really works out pretty well.

I was at a meeting one time with two department store executives that were on a particular board. I got to know them well and visited one who ran a large department store with about a dozen locations in the west. And, I said, "How do you like this department store business, Charlie?"

And he said, "Let me tell you, Milt, it's the toughest business I have ever been in during my life." By the way, this gentleman had been in a lot of developments and other enterprises. Well, about 15 minutes later I saw this other chap who was the executive in another department store. His operation was larger with about 40-50 stores stretching form the Midwest to the West. I asked him the very same question. "Jim, how do you like the department store business?" and he said, "Milt, I love it!" I asked him, "Isn't it a tough business?" He responded that it wasn't, really, that it was a very interesting business, that it was very profitable, and that he never really saw it as a tough business.

That is where I concluded that the first guy was unsure of what he was doing and that the second guy knew everything he needed to know about the business.

So, two guys are in the same business and one says that it is tough and the other says he is very profitable and doing well and he just loves what he is doing. The difference between a business that is tough and one that is easy, is that the latter is the person knows what the hell he is doing and the other doesn't have clue."

In the early years of Horizon, I was invited to a regional airlines meeting and was put on the government relations board. This was my first meeting with other airline presidents. I recall the fellow next to me saying to the person opposite, and I don't recall what airline he was with, "Wouldn't this be a fun business, Charlie, if it wasn't for the passengers?"

Perhaps it was in jest, but it really demonstrated his lack of commitment to service.

The Redmond, Oregon, city bureaucrats wanted to start their own airline; I mean as the bureaucrats. They got together and thought they could start up an airline. Let me tell you something: bureaucrats can't do anything. All they can do is screw up everything that others are doing because that is all they know how to do. The best they can do is screw up something that is already working.

About pilots. I'll admit that perhaps I didn't have a clear understanding of their tasks in the beginning. Prior to takeoff, they are busy pre-flighting their aircraft and checking weather, or whatever else occupies them. Later, I realized that once they are in the air, their responsibilities are ever-present. Just dealing with the air traffic control system and collision avoidance would overwhelm me.

The news media? Well, I upset a few of them. They would ask a question that I would truthfully answer and they wouldn't like it. I don't know why presidential candidates have so much trouble with the press. Why don't they tell them to go stuff it? If a candidate doesn't like a particular question, why don't they say, "I don't answer those dumb questions. Now, I can give you some questions that you could ask me."

I used to do that, telling them not to ask the dumb questions. You know a lot of people in the media are really not very bright. *(There goes our book review!)* Some of them are excellent, others are sad.

I recognize my language needs improvement. You know, I have given some serious thought to expanding this Milt Kuolt Charm School. There are a lot of people I would put through that, including myself!

Given Milt Kuolt's personal dynamics and being a child of missionaries, it has been suggested that he could have been another Billy Graham.

Well, I don't know. I have a friend who calls me Brother Milt and I call him Brother Marjoe. Marjoe Gortner. He was an evangelist from the time he was six years old and he's turned out to be a pretty good friend of mine and we kid about it. I've told him a couple of times that we ought to form a partnership: he would do the preaching and I would take the money and we'd do some good things with it. I said, "We'll just raise millions like those dudes on television." But, it was more of a joke than anything else.

I don't know if many know this, but I may not have turned out like my father expected because I didn't go into the ministry. It is widely recognized that my language would never survive there. Maybe my heart would, but not my personality.

A Message To Garcia

A booklet was given to Milt Kuolt by his parents in 1940 shortly after he and his family arrived in America from India. Entitled "A Message To Garcia," it had a tremendous impact on Milt's outlook and philosophy. Here it is:

When war broke out between Spain and the United States, it was necessary to communicate quickly with the leader of the insurgents. Garcia was somewhere in the mountains of Cuba, no one knew where. No mail or telegraph message could reach him. The President had to secure his cooperation, and quickly. What to do?

Someone said to the President, "There is a fellow by the name of Rowan who will find Garcia for you, if anybody can." Rowan was sent for and given a letter to be delivered to Garcia. Rowen sealed the letter in an oilskin pouch, strapped it over his heart, in four days landed by night off the coast of Cuba from an open boat, disappeared into the jungle, and in three weeks, came out on the other side of the island, having traversed a hostile country on foot and delivered his letter to Garcia.

By the Eternal! *There* is a man whose form should be cast in deathless bronze and the statue placed in every college and university in the land. It is not book-learning young men need, nor instruction about this and that, but a stiffening of the vertebrae which will cause them to be loyal to a trust, to act promptly, concentrate their energies: *do the thing* – carry a message to Garcia!

Slipshod assistance, foolish inattention, dowdy indifference and halfhearted work seem the rule; and no man succeeds unless by hook or crook or threat he forces or bribes other men to assist him; or God, in his goodness performs a miracle and sends him an Angel of Light for an assistant.

You, reader, put this matter to a test: You are sitting now in your office, six clerks are within call. Summon any one and make this request: "Please look in the encyclopedia and make a brief memorandum for me concerning the life of Correggio."

Will the clerk quiety say, "Yes, sir," and go do the task? On your life, he will not. He will look at you out of a fishy eye and ask one or more of the following questions:

Who was he?

Which encyclopedia?

Where is the encyclopedia?

Was I hired for that?

Don't you mean Bismarck?

What's the matter with Charlie doing it?

Is he dead?

Is there any hurry?

Shall I bring you the book and let you look it up yourself?

What do you want to know for?

And I will bet you ten to one that after you have answered the questions and explained how to find the information and why you want it, the clerk will go off and ask one of the other clerks to help him try to find Correggio, then come back and tell you there is no such man.

Now, if you are wise, you will not bother to explain to your "assistant" that Correggio is indexed under C, not K, but you will smile very sweetly and say, "Never mind," and go look it up yourself. And this incapacity for independent action, this moral stupidity, this infirmity of the will, this unwillingness to cheerfully catch hold and live; these are the things to deplore. If men will not act for themselves, what will they do when the benefit of their effort is for everyone?

Nothing is said about the employer who grows old before his time in a vain attempt to get frowsy ne'er-do-wells to do intelligent work and his long, patient striving after "help" that does nothing but loaf when his back is turned. In every store and factory, there is a constant weeding out process going on. The employer is constantly sending away "help" that have shown their incapacity to further the interests of the business and others are being taken on. No matter how good the times, this sorting continues. Only if times are hard and work is scarce is the sorting done finer but out and forever out the incompetent and unworthy go. It is the survival of the fittest. Self-interest prompts every employer to keep the best, those who can carry a message to Garcia.

I know one man of really brilliant parts who has not the ability to manage a business of his own, yet is absolutely worthless to anyone else because he carries with him constantly the insane suspicion that his employer is oppressing, or intending to oppress him. He cannot give orders and he will not receive them. Should a message be given to him to take to Garcia, his answer would probably be, "Take it yourself."

Tonight this man walks the streets looking for work, the wind whistling through his threadbare coat. No one who knows him dares employ him, for his is a regular firebrand of discontent. He is impervious to reason and the only thing that can impress him is the toe of a thick-soled boot.

Of course, I know that one so morally deformed is no less to be pitied than a physical cripple; but in our pitying, let us drop a tear, too, for the men who are striving to carry on a great enterprise, whose working hours are not limited by the whistle and whose hair is fast turning white through the struggle to hold in line dowdy indifference, slipshod imbecility and the heartless ingratitude which, but for their enterprise, others would be both hungry and homeless.

Have I put the matter too strongly? Possibly I have. But when all the world has gone a slumming, I wish to speak a word of sympathy for the man who succeeds; the man who, against great odds, has directed the efforts of others, and having succeeded, finds there is nothing but bare board and clothes. I have carried a dinner pail and worked for a day's wages and I have also been an employer of labor and I know there is something to be said on both sides. There is no excellence, per se, in poverty. Rags are no recommendation and all employers are not rapacious and high-handed, any more than all poor men are virtuous. My heart goes out to the man who does his work when the "boss" is away, as well as when he is at home. After the man who, when given a letter to Garcia, quietly takes the missive, without any idiotic questions and with no lurking intention of chucking it into the nearest sewer. It is one long, anxious search for such an individual.

Anything such a man asks shall be granted. He is wanted in every city, town and village, in every office, shop, store and factory. The world cries out for such. He is needed and needed badly – the man who can carry a Message to Garcia!

Epilogue

To observe the 15th anniversary of Horizon's first flight, members of the original teams gathered in 1996 at Milt and Kathy's *casitas* at Los Flamingos, Puerto Vallarta for a celebration. It was a grand time as fond as well as painful recollections were exchanged.

In planning the get together, Dee Dee and Milt pondered a name for the event, finally settling on "Remember the Magic." Under the *palapa*, beverages and memories flowed equally. One recollection sparked another and so it went, into the night.

El Guapo – "the handsome one," Puerto Vallarta 15th Anniversary occasion in Mexico.

A golf tournament was part of the festivities. The golfers selected caddies from those eager to carry clubs for the *gringos*. Kuolt explained, "They're betting on us. My caddie says that I will

Bruce McCaw, Jamie Milagro, and Dee Dee Maul.

post a better score and your caddie is betting I won't."

Everything went well until the 15th hole when Milt's partner missed a four-foot putt, prompting his caddie to exclaim in perfect English, "Senor, what happened?"

When Milt began to spend more time in Mexico, he brought his Humvee south of the border. The Humvee became recognized around the world as a prominent U.S. military vihicle used in the Gulf War. It has also become recognized in Puerto Vallarta and the villages nearby, with Milt Kuolt behind the wheel. He loads the Humvee with guests at the Los Flamingos enclave and drives wildly down the road, through the villages and onto the beach to demonstrate the vehicle's prowess. At the same time, he brings a little more excitement into the lives of his guests. That's Milt Kuolt. Always ready to do whatever he can for you. And his legion of friends say, "*May he never change.*"

A Last Word on Service

I t appears that many carriers in the new millennium are still not listening to passenger concerns nor are they making "service to the customer" the foundation of their operation. According to a 1998 University of Michigan School of Business Survey, nearly 10,000 formal passenger complaints were filed with the Department of Transportation, a 26 percent surge over the prior year.

The DOT estimates that for every such message they receive, up to 400 are sent along to the offending airline. That translates to as many as 38 million disgruntled air travelers, placing the airlines near the bottom (tied with TV networks) among 34 industries rated for customer satisfaction.

The prosperity of Horizon Air, the regional that made service to the customer the number one goal, coupled with the fortunes of its parent, Alaska, seemed rosy as the

90s wound to a close. Of course, with Horizon Air's growth to a 4,000-plus-employee company, labor relations became more complex than in the early days when the airline had just 36 employees.

In 2001, after lengthy discussions, Horizon negotiated a first contract with its pilots, and the contract appeared headed for approval by the end of the summer.

A Personal Epilogue

Kathy and Milagro

Milt Kuolt remembers how he and Kathy met in 1980 through a mutual friend during one of the outings on Thousand Trails' yacht, the *Shaman*.

"I guess I didn't realize it at the time, but she told me later that she was flirting with me – and I guess most guys don't always perceive this. About a month after we met, I took her to dinner a few times and got to know her better. And I realized she was a real quality gal."

When Kuolt learned she was seeking a full time job, he told Kathy that she should talk with Mike Moyer, a Trails' vice president, about full time employment with the company. Her job in community relations was to follow the marketing team into new communities and smooth out any ruffled feelings. After about two years, Milt got to know

Kathy well and thought *this is the gal I ought to marry.* They really enjoyed each other's company and one day before Horizon was a year old, Milt just matter-of-factly said, "Why don't we just get married?" Milt remembers Kathy's response was "That's a great idea!"

They were married May 26, 1982.

To this day, Dee Dee Maul says she doesn't know how they balanced their diverse personalities, but that the two had "an incredible love affair that was something very special."

"It is not easy for Milt to show his tender emotions, but Kathy dealt with that beautifully," Dee Dee remembers. "They were able to tease and joke with one another. She had a sense of humor and loved to laugh. And that's why Kathy and I were such great friends – she loved my jokes. Even my off-color jokes that I inherited from my father. Kathy and Milt shared their sense of humor with each other. When Milt was really uptight, Kathy could make a statement that would cause him to lighten up."

Close friend, Joyce Adams, remembers the calming effect Kathy had on Milt. "When things got emotional in a business or personal conversation, Kathy would just reach over and slowly rub Milt's arm and settle him down. Milt was the center of Kathy's universe."

Tragedy struck when, shortly after their marriage, Kathy was diagnosed with breast cancer and underwent surgery in 1983. The cancer went into remission, allowing Milt and Kathy to travel with friends and have some memorable, sometimes hilarious times. An example is shared here by Joyce:

"Peter Prabhu, the archbishop of Zimbabwe, is a good friend of Milt's. My husband, David, and I accompanied Milt and Kathy to Zimbabwe. Driving along with the archbishop at the wheel was an exciting experience for me. He would drive pretty fast, dodging in between cars and passing them on any side that was convenient. I was frightened. Milt wouldn't ask him to slow down. Then Milt took a siesta. Seeing in his rear view mirror that Milt was asleep, the archbishop took the opportunity to drive a little faster. We went dodging and weaving for what seemed to me a very long time. I was so uptight, I tried to read a book and pray. I kept looking at Kathy, indicating that I was ready to slug Milt with my book but Kathy gave me a wide-eyed look of consternation that asked, 'How can you be *reading a book* at a time like this?' I concentrated on one thought: *We can't die! He's an archbishop!*

"We arrived safely. Milt woke up, unaware of our harrowing ride. I was shaking so badly that I could hardly talk. But then we just cracked up and started laughing about it with the archbishop. I don't know, maybe it was an automatic release of joy that we had survived the ride."

Fright of another kind was to invade the lives of these good friends in 1992.

"Kathy's heart's desire was to have a baby," Joyce recalls. "It was so important to her. The birth of their daughter, Jamie Milagro, was against all odds, truly a miracle."

Jamie Milagro Kuolt was born on March 28, 1991, the fulfillment of her mother's hopes and dreams. Nine months later, the cancer was back. This time, in the bone.

The battle for Kathy's life began in earnest as doctors, family members and friends came forward to do whatever

Kathy, Milagro, and Milt Kuolt; Puerto Vallarta, 1996.

they could to help. Milt tried to stay busy. He crammed as much joy, as much enrichment into Kathy's life as he possibly could. In between treatments, Kathy rallied to go on happy trips with Milt and good friends.

"The family would come to our ranch in eastern Washington," Joyce remembers. "We had the most wonderful times together. My granddaughter, Lizzie, now ten years old, would be there for Jamie and we laughed a lot and reminisced. Through it all, Kathy was so cheerful, so giving, so courageous, never thinking about herself, but always about others.

"One day she was in a lot of pain and handed me something wrapped in tissue paper. She said, 'I've worn this a lot and I want you to have it.' It was a beautiful gold necklace I will always treasure. I gave her a diamond cross that she cherished. That's the way it was with us."

As it became apparent that treatment was to no avail, Joan Sexton, Kathy's devoted sister, took a leave from her job to be with Kathy. Her other sisters, Linda and Vicki and her brother, Bob, came to comfort. Lenora Boshers, Kathy's mother, also a cancer victim, was vigilant and the one Kathy telephoned on the night before she died. Milt's executive assistant, Sandra Mitchell was a steadfast friend who helped Milt care for Kathy with genuine affection. Nancy Johnson came with spiritual insight and positive thinking that kept Kathy hoping until the end.

"I was with her when she died," Joyce recalls. "I really didn't think she was going to die. I thought we would just continue being best friends forever. Milt cried. He went to Jamie to tell her that her Mommy had died. She was seven years old, this precious, precocious little girl her Mommy had dreamed about. It was the hardest thing Milt ever had to do. It was very hard for all of us who were there. Since then, Milt reminds Jamie daily how much her Mommy loved her.

"Two weeks after Kathy passed away, we were together and Lizzie and Jamie started chanting, 'Wish I may, wish I might, have the wish I wish tonight.'

"And Jamie said aloud that if she looked at the stars enough, she would see her Mommy. I looked into her little face and told her she was part of her Mommy; that Mommy would always be in her heart. That seemed to do the trick. Jamie said, 'You know what? I get it!'

"In the time that has passed, I have seen Jamie express her innate sense of compassion to others who are hurting or in need. She is a special girl. I promised Kathy I would always be there for Jamie.

"At Kathy's service, Father Philip Wallace presented a very special angel statue to Jamie. Father Phil said the angel was to remind Jamie that her Mommy was always watching out for her. Kathy will always be a part of her little girl's life."

Milt Kuolt, intrepid entreprenuer, had been in a battle he could not win. He would raise the light of his life alone, somewhat overwhelmed at age 73, raising a child now almost ten.

Milagro is a polite child with signature red hair who is bilingual, well mannered and very bright. Her name in Spanish translates to *Miracle* because, Milt says, doctors didn't think Kathy could have a child. Candidly he adds, "If I were a young girl that age, I'd be damned if I would want to be raised by a 73-year-old." Following the self-deprecating remark, he hastens to add with a smile that he brings in her friends who live some distance away to play with Milagro. He also arranged during the year 2000 to have Jody Phillips help Milagro with schoolwork and participate in social functions. Family members have also been helpful with many of the things little girls need that he says he doesn't do too well. Milt's grown daughters, Sandy and Suzanne Kuolt come to help. Milt believes Milagro likes the arrangement and he is never too busy to respond when she calls, "Poppy!" to interrupt whatever he is doing.

Months before Kathy passed away, Milt bought her a house in Scottsdale, thinking that the Arizona climate and proximity to the Mayo clinic would be of benefit. She came to visit a couple of times but was unable

to move there permanently. Milt later moved to the house in Scottsdale and enrolled Milagro in school there. She is doing well.

What's That 'Round Your Head?
For over 20 years, this has been Milt's special song to Kathy

What's that 'round your head – Is it a halo?

And what's that on your shoulders – Is it wings?

You must be a walking piece of heaven

Or is it love that makes me see these things?

Round you is a light that keeps on glowing

When you speak do I hear angels sing

You must be a walking piece of heaven

Or is it love that makes me see these things?

When we met you gave me strength

To face the world.

I believe you're special;

You're no ordinary girl.

Am I seeing right or am I dreaming

Do I hear the rush of angels' wings?

You must be a walking piece of heaven

Or is it love that makes me see these things?

Donna Christiansen, one of Horizon's first flight attendants, is still flying with Horizon in 2001.

Horizon Air's Accounting Department Staff, Christmas Day, 1982. Seated are Controller Mike Lowry and Department Manager Bonnie Gustafson. Left to right, standing: Ruth, Lita, Chris, Janell, Helen, Gladys, Trish, Lori, Annie and Judy. Photo taken in the old corporate office at the end of the North-South Runway at SeaTac on 188th Street. (Photo courtesy Lori Moe)

Brenda and Sandy at the Sun Valley Station in 1986.

Simone Irion (center) at the Sun Valley Station in 1987. She is still employed there.

Bill, Alex and Todd at the Sun Valley Station, 1986.

Milt in Mexico

Bruce McCaw, George Bagley and Milt Kuolt with two Horizon pilots.

Kathy Kuolt, Mona Kays, and Milt Kuolt during "Western Party Time."

Boise Station personnel around the time of Alaska's acquisition of Horizon. From left: Janet Drexler, Barry Lane, Mike Waters, Kyle Anderton and Jim Pearl. (Photo courtesy of Janet Drexler.)

HORIZON AIR

HORIZON'S Chairman Says Let's Print an Annual Report People Will Pick Up and Read

de Havilland DASH 8 Heralds Era of Advanced Technology

New Aircraft: Quieter, More Efficient, Economical

In recent years Horizon's President, Milt Kuolt, may have felt like his office was a reception center for the world's aircraft manufacturers. Representatives from several different countries had shown up at Horizon at one time or another hawking their wares.

A wide choice of aircraft is available to a regional airline: twin-engine, four-engine, jet, propjet, you name it. Passenger configurations ranging from twelve to 125 were all presented to Kuolt.

Then, on September 3, 1985 Horizon announced its choice: the de Havilland DHC-8, more popularly known as the "Dash 8", would be the *(continued on page 2)*

Most Are Too Stuffy

SEATTLE—Corporate Offices—The conversation went like this: "It's that time again, Chief, what do you want to do about the Annual Report?"

"What did the one cost last year?" Given the figures, Horizon's chairman and president, Milton G. Kuolt II, said, "That was too much for a report. Why don't we do one on newsprint and give people something that's interesting, informative and one they'll read?

"I personally find most annual reports contain traditionally archaic methods of communicating—lots of words without much meaning, an 'issue' in a newspaper format should have a much higher readership because of its style.

And, that is how you find yourself reading a corporate annual report that is a departure from most corporate annual reports—one done in a newspaper format and,

hopefully, interesting enough that you'll stay with it through the less-than-exciting financials to learn what this airline is all about.

Milt's Philosophy on Regional Airlines & Horizon

"If anyone thinks that all it takes to create a successful airline is some airplanes and a compelling desire to fly, they're going to be sadly disillusioned," Milt Kuolt says. "An overwhelming compulsion to fly airplanes does not guarantee success.

These remarks are characteristic of the carrier's chief executive officer as he cites his philosophy for the regional airline industry. With nearly five years of industry experience under his belt Kuolt feels comfortable about citing the industry's ills and he isn't shy about saying what he believes caused Horizon's red ink in 1985 either.

"We had too many things diverting our attention into non-operational areas in 1985; away from the internal disciplines of planning, systems and cost control.

"Frankly, we reached a period of growth where we outstripped management's combined capabilities." *(continued on page 6)*

Sr. VP Peare Cites 1986 As Year To "Get Better Not Bigger"

Operations to Get Special Attention

The way Bill Peare, Senior V.P. of Operations tells it, Horizon's passengers are going to benefit along with the company's employees in 1986 as the operations area gains special attention.

"Programs are going into place in 1986 that will allow each station manager to develop ways to better serve our passengers," Peare said.

"A key point in this program is to set up our Seattle station as a training center to initiate and prove systems here before they're implemented at the various stations."

Greater emphasis on passenger service will be an essential element in this plan for 1986. Peare says that the airline will be exploring ways to have closer-in gates at the various cities it serves—for example, where passengers

can benefit from one-stop ticketing and can check and pick up baggage more quickly and conveniently than in the regular baggage claim areas.

"We want to eliminate *(continued on page 2)*

CONTENTS

TOP 10 REGIONAL AIRLINES IN 1984

1984 RANK	CARRIER	1984 PASSENGERS	1983 RANK
• 1.	Mid Pacific Airlines	1,338,284	1
• 2.	PBA	1,331,491	3
3.	Britt Airways	1,204,885	2
• 4.	Air Wisconsin	1,095,000	4
• 5.	Empire Airlines	1,073,452	5
• 6.	Metro Airlines	844,839	7
• 7.	Horizon Airlines	769,625	11
• 8.	Mississippi Valley Airlines	741,279	8
9.	Henson Airlines	733,536	6
• 10.	Air Midwest	710,782	16

• Denotes Public Ownership

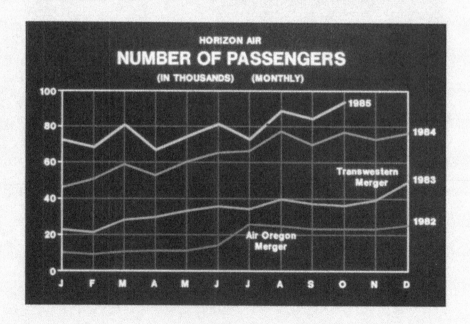

HORIZON AIR
NUMBER OF PASSENGERS
(IN THOUSANDS)   (MONTHLY)